Slices of Life

Slices of Life

Jagmit Singh

DIGITALSPINES

First Edition, 2023

Instagram: @blogs.dialogues

Paperback ISBN: 978-81-977702-7-2
eBook ISBN: 978-81-19221-88-2
WebPDF ISBN: 978-81-19221-93-6

Published by DIGITAL SPINES.
Originally published by 16Leaves.

I dedicate this book to my grandfather (Bauji) S. Indar Singh jee, and my parents S. Pritam Singh jee and Mrs. Vidushi Pritam Singh. Though they are no more physically with us, their blessings will always be with me. I am what I am all because of them and I am sure they would be proud that I wrote a book.

I would like to thank my immediate family, Preeti, my wife, Arshiya my daughter and Naunidh my son in law and my sisters Jasleen and Manjula for their support and encouragement. A special mention to my cousin Puneet for motivating me.

My thanks also to my close friends from college (SRCC, New Delhi) Denzil and Chandan.

Special thanks to friends Ambassador Manjeev S Puri and his wife Namrita.

I would like to thank my entire batch of Modern School (The Together Forever 1976!)
In particular Radhika, Nita, Dr Harsh, Deepak Rana and Pradeep Bahl.

My entire group of Table Tennis friends from Saket Sports Complex New Delhi.

I cannot forget to thank all my Facebook Friends and Air India Colleagues too for their constant encouragement. Ambassador Deepa Gopalan Wadhwa and (Juju Chachiji) Mrs Jyotsana Singh for always appreciating my attempts at poetry.

A special thanks to Cecil and Darlene for always encouraging and motivating me.

My thanks are due to 16Leaves, the Publishers for without them, this book would not be in existence.

Most of all my thanks and gratitude to Almighty God as everything is possible only with His grace and blessings.

Foreword

I must have met Jagmit sometime in 2004, when I moved to live in Gurgaon and went to Saket DDA sports complex, some sixteen kilometers away, to play table tennis. Every Sunday. And sometimes on Saturday morning before going to office in Safdarjung Enclave which must have been seven kilometers. Those were the days when my wife used to say I was married more to table tennis than to her. There might have been something to it. Before I moved to Gurgaon, I lived in Green Park Extension and went every Sunday with Bunty to the DDA sports complex near GTB Hospital in Ghaziabad to play table tennis, and that was twenty-seven kilometers away. It took more than an hour to get there even. I was away, needless to say, for most of the day, and when I got back home, I'd find that in the pecking order of life, the wife came below table tennis, work, jazz downloads, alcohol. It is not that it would have been difficult to find a table to play nearer where I lived around

Gurgaon. It is just that it is not easy find people like Jagmit, Bunty, R K Sharma, Dr Sagar, Salil, Vikram, or Sujoy, to play table tennis with. I don't play a competitive game, it was recreational. Jagmit, I found, put up an impregnable wall of defence most days, and no matter how swiftly I sent the Nitaku premium ball cracking, Jagmit would send it back, and wait for me to tire or make mistakes, smiling his angelic smiles with his missing teeth and hugging me fiercely after the game. He is a fierce hugger.

I never asked him about his teeth and how and where he had lost them. That would have been too personal. I never asked him how he played so well either. We lived in the moment, in that bubble, and the only thing that mattered was how you spurred the ball to the other side. Many times, that moment lasted from seven in the morning till three in the afternoon when even the sun had begun to tire, and as the day wore on, we would grow younger and younger, drinking tea and eating pakoras between games, and squabble like children over every point. It is only now when I read the manuscript of poetry prose that Jagmit sent me, that I came to know how he lost so many teeth and in one go, and I also learnt how he came to have this defensive game: his formative racket was Double Happiness, which table tennis lovers will immediately understand as a valid underpinning for defence. Nor did I know that Jagmit was briefly under the tutelage of Thangavelu Thiruvengadam, a national player with a defensive bent of game. Nor that he is an inveterate sportsman, be it squash, badminton but not swimming, especially not swimming. You will have to read this book to find out why. I wish he had kept the prose portion a little longer but if wishes were BMW X1 third hand, I'd be driving one.

Jagmit discovered the joys of writing much later in life. Here, he exhibits a light touch, sometimes tender, sometimes rueful, reflective, sometimes mischievous, sweetly nostalgic, when he writes of days where.. Na TV Tha, Na AC/Panee to nal se hee bharte the/Bahut Acheche the who din", but always positive. As he says perhaps his blood group has something to do with it. Not many aspects of life escape his ruminative scrutiny, starting from his grandfather, working his way down to his mother, his father with the beautiful handwriting, his wife, daughter, spilling arresting images along the way. I'd almost forgotten what a hold-all was till Jagmit reminded me of one that looked like a "fat Punjab Police cop." I wonder if I could have ever gone for a five to six am slot in Nanak Pura to play table tennis, especially in Delhi winters. But I now know that if I had met Jagmit back in the day and he asked me to I would. Without hesitation.

V Sudarshan

He is a renowned journalist and has worked in various publications. Indian Express, Pioneer, Outlook, New Indian Express and The Hindu. He has authored the following, Anatomy of an Abduction, Adrift, Dead-end, Tuticorin. He likes Jazz, Table-tennis and Alcohol, though not necessarily in that order! Recently he has discovered Crime writing and Crime fiction.

Contents

PROSE

Myself

I am going to write about myself, it's a subject I know about personally and since I've already experienced more than 64 years on this beautiful planet, I would like to share my thoughts and experiences and perhaps the readers might appreciate some part of what I've written and maybe benefit in some way.

I'm a simple person and blessed to be born as the third child of my parents into a Sikh family in the spring of 1959. My name is Jagmit Singh which in my language means world friend. I was a shy and a little plump child, fair in looks and since I had long hair and looked different from others, other children would make fun of me. Of course, I didn't like it but there wasn't much I could do about it.

I was a below average student and studied in a school run by Christian Missionary school till the Fourth class. Since we were four of us children at home, my eldest brother five years older than me and my two sisters one two years elder and the other two years younger, we were never lonely and used to play and fight all the time.

My parents were the best persons I could have asked for. When I was 7 or 8 years old my father got transferred to Kathmandu, Nepal for a three-year posting and all of us relocated except my elder brother who was in a senior class and my parents felt shifting moving him might affect his education.

In a way those three plus years were a golden period in my life. The education standard was not so high and very soon I started becoming a topper in my class. Since my brother was not around, I was more carefree as he used to bully me at times. I was quite independent too and used to move around freely on a bicycle, going to school as well as meeting my friends. Till this time, I was more or

less an ordinary happy child who hadn't committed many sins except for a few occasions of stealing some money so as to be able to fly kites on my own as my brother didn't allow me and also stealing some stamps from my grandfather's spectacle case.

Both these incidents were found out and I felt very bad and miserable after that.

Another thing I did in my school in Kathmandu was to steal a lot of stamps from the principals room. One day, since I felt the pressure of being a topper I also tried to cheat at an exam. We moved back to India and I joined a school mid-session and it was very difficult for me to adjust to the higher standards of education in Delhi. I started picking up and then was very upset as my parents put me into a more reputed school where I did not want to go.

In this new school there was not much discipline and so I never applied myself and got poor marks in my final school board exams which left me very unhappy and I started blaming my parents for it, that they changed my school so many times.

I joined a college, a prestigious college as even though I had not done as well as I should have, I still had a first division. The college years were traumatic. I initially wished to redeem myself by excelling to make up for what I considered poor marks in school. Whatever be the reason, I fared miserably in college and for the first time in my life I failed. This affected my self-esteem so much; I went into a depression and avoided meeting people. Amongst my family and friends, no one had failed. I started blaming my college, that the lecturers were not good and all of us who took up economics honours were first divisioners however most of us after the first year of college ended up as third divisioners.

During this time of increased freedom, I took to certain bad habits. At home due to my age there was not much that my parents could do to discipline me. They were very sweet anyway and tolerated my every kind of behaviour.

Those years made a very big impact on my life. My peers and friends moved on in life achieving excellence at academics, became doctors, engineers and chartered accountants while I was at a standstill. Many avenues were blocked for me. I was unemployed for a long time and my parents were very worried about my future. Finally, I got a job! My general knowledge was good and that helped. It was not an officers' job, but it was with a reputed Airlines. Three years after my job I got

married. After a further three-year period we had a child. Today I'm a retired person. As I look back on my past, I feel a big sense of gratitude. I now am a firm believer in the Almighty. By the grace of God today I have everything, a home, my wife, a beautiful daughter and a nice son in law. We have more than enough for our needs. Two adorable grandsons who are twins. There was a time I used to think, what will become of me, I don't have a job, who will marry me, all friends and peers are doing so much better than me. Now however since I started believing in God, and I have realized my mistakes and feel sorry for all my wrong acts and ask for forgiveness from God, I am quite content. I look around me and see beauty everywhere! I am able to forgive myself for my mistakes and move forward in life as also I am able to forgive others who in my perception have not been good or done right to me. The reason is simple, I'm not perfect myself so I have no right to judge others. I find that I get great solace in adhering to what my religion teaches me. It says remember God always, thank Him for everything, do not be too attached to anybody or with worldly things like wealth, family etc, we are just like guests here and the only thing which we can take back with us are our good acts and deeds and God's name. It is best to try and control your mind and overcome the 5 deadly demons like kaam, krodh, lobh, Moh and ahankar or Lust, Anger, Greed, Attachment and pride or ego.

If we can do that, we will be in a permanent phase of Anand or bliss. That is what God wants us to be. To be happy.

Thus, to sum up I would say, Life is quite short, enjoy the moments, in everyone's life there will be both joys and sorrows, pain and happiness. Be Equanimical and know that no time is permanent. This too shall pass, have faith in God and try to do the right thing. Be nice to people, keep your word, look after your body and mind.

Don't give anyone the power to affect your happiness or to try and control you.

Look at the positive side of things, there is always so much to be grateful for.

Mama

If there is an inspiring story about women to be told, the person who comes to mind is my mother - Mrs Vidushi Pritam Singh. Sadly, she is no more with us; she passed away a few years ago at the age of 82.

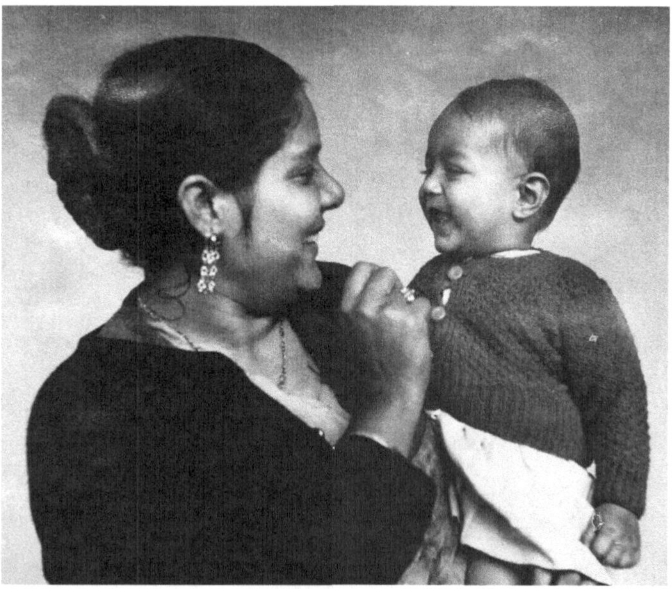

She was the daughter of a respected civil engineer who was a senior government officer. She had a happy childhood and was fond of music, painting and dance, though not very studious! The youngest in her family, she'd lived a comfortable life - with bearers serving dinner with fancily arranged cloth napkins.

She was an extremely talented artist though didn't pursue it after getting married. There is an interesting anecdote of her childhood. One day she told her mother, please buy me a garland. When her mother questioned why, she said, today the result is being declared and if I pass, I will garland my teacher. What if you fail, her mother asked "then I will put it on myself!"

When she came back from school, she was wearing the garland! She was jovial, as can be seen from the above instance!!, and used to fondly relate this incident to us and later to her grandchildren too!

As was the custom then, she was married when she was 20. Her husband, Mr Pritam Singh, was exceptionally bright and had joined the same office as her father. By the age of 28, she had four children.

When she got married, she moved into her husband's house which was a totally different environment from where she lived previously. There were no servants. It was a small flat full of a lot of people. Partition had happened and a lot of people were accommodated as they had no other place to stay. Here there was no dining table, leave aside napkins!

She toiled hard, with a smiling face, and got along well with her parents- in-law, brother-in-law and family. Though I never met my grandmother, as she expired before I was born, my mother always used to praise her a lot. She was known as Bhabijee.

My mother raised the four of us and instilled good values in us. You can well imagine how much hardship she had to undergo looking after her husband and a large family.

As my father rose in his service, my mother started getting more comforts, like the help of a servant and a car at her disposal.

We used to live in government flats, and my mother being very sociable and the only lady in the neighbourhood who knew how to drive a car, would always ask the other ladies when she had to go shopping. They would happily accompany her and do their shopping too! That's the kind of person she was, helpful and generous.

Strong, confident and determined, she was brave and always cheerful. She was a do gooder and loved sharing helpful information. Unfortunately, she expected the same from others, to give selflessly, which often didn't happen.

Her optimism and positive attitude opened doors, made her always try. An example being, parking spots emerged for her even though my father said "you will not find parking! ".

She really didn't care what others would think of her, In those days there were very few cars on the road and hardly any women drivers. I remember she used to visit her grandmother, who was living in Gandhi Colony (across the Yamuna), whereas we used to live in South Delhi so it was a fair distance away, and once we entered the colony young children would see her driving and get excited by the sight of a woman driver! They used to chase our car.

My father was posted to Kathmandu in the year 1966 or so, and he bought a second-hand white Mercedes car, which of course my mother would drive too. It so happened, once there was a car rally going on, and there were crowds along the road, my mother had stepped out in the car, and people cheered her too! Thinking she is a contestant!

There are so many examples of her goodness, she had gone to visit my sister in USA, and per chance came to know that a school friend of mine was getting married in the Gurdwara, she volunteered to help and made langar (food) for the wedding party! She used to cook for my sister while in America.

She loved distributing her jams and achars to friends and relatives who she knew enjoyed them.

That's the kind of person she was, happy, sociable, helpful and an optimist. Reality of Words Publication

She always saw the positive side in everything and was very God fearing. I remember vividly she would do the evening prayer „ Rahras saab" even though she was driving or anywhere, and we would listen in silence. Over the years this led to us also being able to remember the prayer.

She loved helping people and accompanied many of our relatives to visit their loved ones who were hospitalised. She was friendly and approachable. I have not seen her declining anybody for help when approached, if she could, she would help. In any case she lent a sympathetic ear.

She was enterprising too, once I remember she tried her hand at business along with her friend! They used to make frocks and sell to the retailers, unfortunately that venture did not prove to be successful.

She was good at knitting and embroidery and stitched cardigans for her husband and children. She had joined cooking classes and made the most delicious chutneys, pickles and other delectable culinary delights! She was adept at baking and turned-out delicious desserts.

She passed through many hurdles in her life. My father wasn't well and she managed everything by herself. In the early seventies my father was posted out of Delhi as he was chief engineer of a project in Himachal Pradesh. She single handedly got our house constructed during those difficult years, besides managing the house and school going children.

I will describe an instance of her courage during this period. The time the house was being built, everything was strictly rationed and one needed permits for everything. Cement was especially scarce. One night, middle of the night actually, it may have been 3 am, I was sleeping on the first floor of the annexe, (two small living units had been constructed on top of two garages) where we used to stay, the first floor was where I slept, and my two sisters and mother slept on the second floor. The main house was being constructed while we stayed on the site. This is the year 1970 and the place is Vasant Vihar, New Delhi. That time Vasant Vihar was just like a jungle. So suddenly I got up at about 3 am and there was a burly six-foot man and he asked where is your mother. I got scared, thinking how did he get in, then discovered later that he had come in through the window. I just said upstairs and promptly locked the door as he went out! A very cowardly act! then I heard sounds and he had rapped on the second floor flat. My mother hearing the sounds got up and asked..who is it!.. And the man, who was drunk got some sense into him, he was an employee (chowkidar) of a neighbouring house and wanted cement bags. Since he was drunk, he committed this act. He came to his sense when my mother spoke to him in a stern voice. And he realised his mistake!

She was always very supportive. I remember I had failed in college and was very depressed. She used to cheer me and say, don't worry! Failures are the pillars of success!

Later in life she enjoyed playing bridge. She was extremely loyal and never forgot the good acts which others had done to her, she would visit elderly relatives and friends even if she was herself unwell at times.

She also always followed her routine, walking, doing path(prayers), supervision of vegetables, groceries, sorting and packing woollen clothes etc. Due to her friendly and helpful nature, she bonded well with relatives from my father's side of the family and my father, who was quite an introvert, also got close to them.

Wisdom in her proverbs. A stitch in time saves nine, Hath pair hilana painda, you have to make - make an effort. In her room she had stuck up a poster. Never, never give up!

She never let any of us feel less loved, even though at times we felt she favoured her first born.

She was very fair to her children and as per her will, she gave us children equally. For her children she would do anything! She was one of the most hospitable persons I have known. Whenever I would visit her, she would tell me, please have some snacks, help yourself from the fridge. This was even when she herself was lying down in the bed.

Towards the end, she suffered too, she had been afflicted by dengue at the age of about 80 and needed to be hospitalised and from that she never recovered fully. She also got Parkinson's disease and suffered from diabetes and high blood pressure.

Towards the end she had to be hospitalised and had to undergo a major surgery, this took its toll.

To sum up I will say this, all mothers are nice, my mother was exceptionally nice and for us, she would do anything. Her presence was a source of strength for all of us.

Dear Mama, words are inept to describe you…I am sure you are smiling down at us. From Heaven.

I will end by writing a few lines of a poem I had written.

> My Mother comes to mind.
> Busy she was.
> With household chores...
> Or just being nice...
> To friends and relatives...
> And playing bridge
> Added to her joy
> She loved taking care

Of her children husband and friends
She had so much joy in her heart
That she"s left some of that in us
At the expense of her health...
She still wanted to take us out for lunch...

Pitaji

Dear Pitaji,
This is a letter to you. And about you.
You are not in this world today. But you will always live in my heart.
I know you are with Got. And since everything is possible with God.
Who knows. Perhaps you might read it!
It is a small write up, about you.

Appended below:

"My Father Sardar Pritam Singh jee!

He was very honest, intelligent, and humble, he didn't speak much, he was a topper

throughout school and college. He was good at all the subjects, and in Engineering,

he broke the record. His name and photograph were published in the newspaper!

He is my hero; he had a beautiful handwriting! He was very loving, he used to take a

lot of interest in all his children's school books which he used to cover so well.

He looked after his clothes very well, his almirah was always so neat. The way he

folded his shirts it seemed as if they had just been ironed.

He was very handsome and was a good swimmer.

I remember my parents used to take us for walks within the colony and he would

point out the stars and show us the constellations.

He was very patient, and in my childhood. I remember getting terrible ear aches.

And I used to scream in pain. And he would take me to the dispensary, the

person on duty would sort out the issue. By flushing out the wax in my ears,

syringing them with water. It was not nice. But it solved the problem. All this would

normally happen late at night!

He loved me a lot. He played badminton with me and I enjoyed playing with him!

So many fond memories of him! Once he told me "Don't do anything. Which you

would be ashamed to tell me! "Actually, I did a lot which I would be ashamed to

tell!

He told me, when he had gone to USA on scholarship. He was a bachelor at the

time. He told me. He had all the freedom and the opportunity to do anything.

However, his thought was, „I wanted my wife to be a virgin, how could I not be pure

myself. "

I used to love it. When I had done well and got a good report. I used to snuggle by him in bed. And we used to go through the report. How proud I used to feel! He used to teach us by example. He never used to spend on himself. He wasn't fond of shopping for himself! He used to say. Waste now. Want not.

He was very wise and due to his wise investments and guidance that all of us children are living comfortably!

My Father never used to talk ill about anybody! He never indulged in gossip or loose talk.

He was respected by all. He will always remain my hero!!"

Thank you Pitaji!

I am nowhere near you. Even if I can be five percent of you, I would have achieved a lot! I am sorry to have caused you pain, and I am sorry for all the mistakes and sins I have committed.

Lots and lots of love!

Your son, Jagmit

Bauji

There are two people in the world, I admire and respect. So much! My Father. Sardar Pritam Singh jee.. And my grandfather. Sardar Indar Singh jee whom we used to call Bauji.

Bauji was so simple. So good. And so religious. He didn't speak much. He was very keen that we grandchildren should learn doing Path (prayers).

He lived alone as my grandmother had expired many years ago. Even before I was born.

One day. I told him..."Bauji..tussi bahut acchey ho"..Which means..Bauji you are very nice. He didn't like me saying than. So nice and humble he was. He told me. I can never forget his reply.."main nahin accha..Rab Accha hai!" Meaning. I am not nice or good. God is good! That"s the kind of person. Never complaining. Content and satisfied. Speaking little.

Another instance I can never forget. I used to be fond of collecting stamps. And he used to give me old stamps. One day. I saw some stamps in his spectacle case. They were a nice pink red colour. I wanted those. He didn't give me. He told me. They are not postage stamps. But revenue stamps. I didn't know the difference. And I wanted them. I stole a few. He found out and told me...you shouldn't have done that I told you they are not postage stamps...I felt very bad. And ashamed.

Another time I remember. I was very small. Maybe in the 2nd or 3d class. And outside our school"s gate.. Columba"s at that time. There were many peddlers who sat on the ground and sold stuff. This man was selling rubbers.. erasers..and there was a big crowd of students in front of him...there were so many rubbers there. And as there was a big crowd. I got tempted and picked up a fistful and went and sat in the bus. Bauji used to stay with us those days. And he saw many rubbers with me.

And asked. How I got them. When I told him. He was very hurt and sad. And he told me..return them tomorrow. The next day. I went near the peddler and there was a crowd as usual. I didn't have the guts to tell the peddler what I had done. But I had wrapped the rubbers in paper. I just threw them. In the pile of rubbers on the floor.

And made my way!

Travel the Perfect Freedom

Perhaps I was born with wheels under my feet!

I was just six months old, when I took my first flight! Of course, I don't remember it, as it was way back in 1959! This is from what my mother had told me, they travelled from Delhi to Srinagar and I must have been in her lap!

From then to now, more than sixty years, I have travelled quite a bit, mostly for pleasure and at times on work.

As a child I remember, we used to travel by train. Those were the days of holdalls! It was like a sturdy bed cover with straps and hooks and you could put anything into it! It just had to be rolled up and then the straps fastened. If, overfull, it would look like a fat Punjab police cop, and if it was less full, it would look sleek, like a gentleman.

It would be fun peering out of the window, watching the countryside flit by and when the train would stop at a station seeing the activity of the hawkers saying „Chai..chai..chai lelo.. chaya Chaya..and imitating them!"

Now my mother used to talk about the number of robberies that took place on trains, especially at night. As I was one of four children and a male, the lower berths would go to my parents or the girls. My elder brother and me, had to sleep on the top berths!

I would have been in the age group of 4 to 8 years during the journeys I am describing, and in my mind, was this fear, of a robber coming and it was scary! So, I used to stay awake, while the train chugged along in the night. Until I was so exhausted that I might sleep, a few hours!

But it was exciting and fun, during the day, we would play cards, and have alu ke parathas with achar, prepared by my mother. These journeys were overnight journeys from Delhi to Calcutta (now Kolkata), or a journey to Bombay (now Mumbai).

Dehradun

We travelled a lot by car too, from Delhi to Dehradun as my grandparents had a big house in Dehradun. Most summer vacations, our family and two of our uncle"s families would go there for a vacation. My Nanaji (grandfather) had built a huge house in Clementown which had open areas, including buffaloes, dogs and a swimming pool too! My Nanaji had expired when I was quite small, but my grandmother used to be there. It was good fun, with all the children, about 10 in all, sleeping on the floor on gaddas (mattresses) in the drawing room.

The ages ranging from 5 to 12 with more girls than boys, as my uncle had 5 daughters. Their Alsatian dog 'Whiskey" was huge, almost as tall as me and we used to throw a rock and he would run and fetch it back! It was fun!

One thing which was of great discomfort for me was, when I had to go for the big job! This was because back home in Delhi, I would always go to the Indian style toilet in our house, and I could not possibly use the western style commode! Then my grandmother found a way out! She said you sit on the commode as if it were an Indian style facing the wall and hold the pipe for support! That's how I used to manage!

We used to go up to Mussoorie too from Dehradun and it used to be fun! Horse-riding, roller skating, eating out at restaurants and eating chooran! Besides of course having great fun playing cards with cousins.

Helambu, Nepal

Another memorable trip was a trek with my father when I was about 12 years old from Kathmandu to a place in the mountains called Helambu. My father was posted in Nepal in the late sixties. It was a seven-day trek and we had porters too.

My father had taken special permission from my school so that I could accompany him. I was a very fair, slightly plump, male Sikh boy and used to tie a patka (head gear), a kind of a mini turban to cover my head. I remember we used to walk all day, and I used to get so tired, that I would just sit down on the track on a stone, saying I'm not walking anymore! But then after some rest and coaxing I had to walk on. The porter would say, we are almost there! We used to stay in the huts or dwellings of the local people as there were no rest houses or other accommodation. At one point, the local people asked my father, Keta cha ki Katy? Nepalese for is it a boy or a girl? Asking about me, since I looked different from them and I had rosy cheeks, they were not quite sure! My father asked, why do you want to know, and the man said, I wanted to get him married to my daughter! I don't know if he was serious or kidding! Child marriages in that region might have been common!

Another vivid instance on that trip was, almost at the end of our journey, we had to cross a river, which was hundreds of feet below, between two mountains and the only way to cross was, by walking on a single piece of wooden plank suspended by ropes, which would also sway with the breeze! I was scared and my father said, can you do it, I thought to myself, there is no other option! With some fear in my heart, slowly I crossed, and made sure I did not look down at the raging river, way below!

Later we met some American ladies, who might have seen, and they remarked, we did not do it! It was a proud and a challenging achievement!

Air India

My first job, rather my only job was with Air India, where I joined, way back in 1983. One of the perks of this job was that we used to get rebated tickets for travel for self and family. In 1984 after completing one year of service, I was raring to go!

My mother and I first flew to London, stopped there a few days and went to New York and to lots of places with the US! We went to Chicago, Boston, Washington and Los Angeles.

We used to stay everywhere with friends or relatives as we could not afford to stay at hotels. As our tickets were subject to availability of seats, we could only travel once all paid passengers had checked in and if seats were still available. An upshot of this was that on the first leg of the journey, Delhi to London, we had to try three times and only on our third attempt we managed seats. It was quite frustrating, waiting till the last moment and then going home. Only to try again!

My mother proudly told her friend and relatives ' in all my years of my husband's service, he could not afford to take me abroad, not counting Nepal of course, and within a year of my son's service, I have been to UK and USA! This would of course make my chest swell up with pride!

At London, my mother insisted I buy and expensive woollen suit from C and A, a big store, in fact I wore the same suit when I got married, a few years later. I still have that suit and it is in great condition!

It was a thrilling experience flying on a Jumbo Jet, with my mother by my side. Later I did many such trips as we tried to use our quota of discounted tickets.

Europe

I will relate an interesting experience which happened in the year 1985, my younger sister, Manjula and me travelled to Europe, we took the Air India flight to Frankfurt and we had fixed up with my friend who lived in Bonn, then the capital of West Germany. My friend worked in the Indian Foreign Service and we expected that he would be there at Frankfurt Airport to meet us. We waited and waited and there was no sign of him, then we got a message from the Air India office that he could not come and would only be available the next day. We were stuck and did not know what to do. Then we thought let us call our fathers German friend who lived in Germany, but we didn't exactly know where. We were carrying his phone number and luckily, he recognized us, and we explained our predicament. He was very nice, and said don't worry, stay wherever you are, and I will come to pick you up. After two hours or so, he came and we went to Karlsruhe, that"s where he stayed.

We spent the night there and then the next day we took the train to Munchen (Munich) and saw the beautiful stadium where the Olympic Games had been held.

Some youngsters were playing music there and there was a huge audience enjoying their music! We soaked in the atmosphere and enjoyed the music too!

We then took the train to Bonn to connect with my friend who had told us he would pick us up from the train station. We were delighted to see him as we got off the train. He took us to his flat.

He was unmarried and had made excellent chicken for us. He told us that we were welcome to stay at his flat for a few days. He had made a program with his office colleague to travel in the car around Europe, Paris and Geneva. He gave us a choice, either stay at my flat till I come back, or accompany me on the Europe trip. It didn't take us long to make the decision!

The next morning the three of us in one car, with my friend at the wheel, and his colleague, who was much elder than us along with his wife and two children, in another car went on our Europe trip!

It was an eventful journey, Mr Harbans Singh and family were in front, and we were behind sitting comfortably listening to English music. My friend, Manjeev put on the news, and we were shocked to hear that Air India Aircraft

Kanishka had crashed! All passengers and crew were feared killed.

We were cruising along when we noticed the car in front suddenly veered right, hit the railing by the edge of the road and stopped. We stopped too and went to their car. Luckily no one was hurt, but the car was damaged and in no condition to make it to Paris! We had already crossed over to France. Along the highway there are phones which are meant for just such a purpose, luckily my sister, Manjula knew a smattering of French as she had done a French course at Alliance Francaise, de Delhi. She picked up the emergency phone and soon the French Police arrived, and then they said, you will have to call for a mechanic. The result was we had to spend the night, huddled in cars on the highway instead of a hotel to Paris!

But these things happen and are part of the excitement and uncertainty of travel! We were relieved to reach Paris! The next morning! We did the regular sightseeing! Eiffel Tower, Arc de Triumph, The Louvre, walked along Champs es lysee. Then we went on to Geneva. My sister and me stayed at a youth hostel on bunk beds! I was in the Gents wing and my sister in the lady"s wing.

The lake in Geneva was beautiful with a huge water jet or fountain soaring high! Then we took a train to Lausanne and Luzerne and saw the breath-taking beauty of Switzerland! At Luzerne there was a very large lake and there was a hedge which was a maze. We got into the maze, but it was with some difficulty that we managed our way out!

Kashmir

In 1986 I got married to Preeti, for our honeymoon we went to Srinagar. We travelled by Indian Airlines as we could use their flights and they ours, something called an interline agreement.

It was a memorable experience as I had booked a holiday home at Srinagar and at Pahalgam. We did all the things that honey- mooners do! Seeing the sights, the Dal Lake, the Shikaras, the lovely Nishat Gardens etc.

We had a cottage to ourselves at Hotel Nedous in Srinagar, all at the price of something like Rs. 12 a day! It was a facility provided by Air India to its employees.

At Pahalgam too we had nice accommodation, though not as luxurious. We even went to Khilanmarg and did some sledding. Or sliding on the ice ..all this in the month of July!

I remember vividly, it was on our honeymoon that we had our first fight! And sulked. She wanted to buy gifts for my side of the family and I felt, it is our honeymoon, it is best to spend and enjoy!

Making friends and trip to Germany

I am going to relate another interesting travel related story. It so happened I was on my way back from Bombay (now Mumbai) to Delhi, after completing an official training course. The year was 1990 I think, and I had boarded the aircraft and was waiting for it to take off, but the plane was stationery, and it was hot and humid, the cabin was not air-conditioned. Nearby there was a foreigner sitting who too was feeling the heat, and was fanning himself with the inflight magazine, I was doing the same exercise with my newspaper.

We got talking and I discovered he had just come from Germany some days ago and had a bad experience at Bombay during his short stay, someone stole his camera. I felt bad, as it left a poor impression of India and Indians. I asked him what is your plan while in Delhi, he replied, ' I will stay a night in Delhi then I am going trekking to the Himalayas and will come back after a week and fly back to Germany.

I asked him, where will you be staying in Delhi? And he said any moderate hotel, so I said why don't you stay with me. He gladly accepted. Rudolph was working as a judge in Berlin and was onsiderably older than me, I was in my early thirties and he was in his fifties. Anyway, he stayed with us for a night, and went to the Himalayas and came back and stayed with us a few days more before going back to Germany. It so happened that after a few months, we, my wife Preeti, daughter Arshiya, who was about 3 years old and me decided to visit my sister in Washington, we travelled by Panam, we had a lovely time with her and on our way back to India, the plane stopped at Frankfurt. I had connected with Rudolph, earlier and he said why don't you have a short stay in Germany, be my guest and then go back to Delhi. We got off at Frankfurt Airport, and we had heavy baggage with us, as my sister had wanted us to carry some of her stuff back to India.

We expected Rudolph to be at the Airport, but we couldn't find him anywhere! Here we were with a small baby and lots of luggage, in a strange country where we did not know anyone. Then after waiting a long time, there was an announcement for me, that someone is waiting for you at the meeting point. We heaved a sigh of relief to find Rudolph there.

He suggested, leave the heavy bags at the Left luggage counter and you can pick them up on your way back. We were so tired after our long journey, so he suggested that we go and stay overnight with his married daughter who lived near Frankfurt.

Rudolph had come in his Audi car to pick us up from Berlin which was at least a two-hour drive. We drove at high speed, but the car was so good, we didn"t feel it. Rudolph opened the sunroof and asked us to put our hand out, and we felt the strength of the wind. We were driving at a speed of over 100 mph!

It was lovely to be hosted by a local German family. I wanted to use the washroom, I was shown the toilet, to my surprise there was no arrangement to lock the toilet from inside! This was usual I believe in that part of the world for families with small children. Rudolph had two sweet grandchildren. I still remember his son in law had done the interiors of the small flat all by himself. In these countries labour is so expensive, most people try to do their work themselves. As we left their house Rudolph"s daughter presented us a jar of homemade jam.

The next morning, he drove us to see the beautiful Cologne cathedral, and on the way, we saw the famous Black Forest too. The countryside was beautiful, and the Cathedral was simply amazing! The beautiful, coloured glass work, the so tall ceiling and the atmosphere of peace was beautiful.

While driving to Berlin, suddenly Rudolph stopped the car and picked up an empty tin of coke which he saw on the road and put it in his car. After driving a bit, he saw a petrol pump and put the tin in the trash can! This is the extent of love for iliness that the Germans have for their country!

We spent two nights with Rudolph and his girlfriend Roswitha in their huge Berlin house. They took us around the sights in Berlin including the Berlin wall which had been demolished after the reunification of East and West Germany. It was a historic place and we saw for ourselves the huge disparity between the houses, roads and other infrastructure. East Germany was far inferior in all these respects as compared to West Germany.

After a wonderful two days spent with our German friends, Rudolph told me that he would not drop us by car to Frankfurt Airport but instead he would put us on the train which would take us straight to the Airport. He said, here is a gift for you! He had been clicking photographs of us from his camera, he had got them developed and that was our gift! Rudolph had been so nice to us that he made us stay in his own bedroom, while Roswitha and he stayed in another room, just to make us feel comfortable! There are so many beautiful memories of our travels to various places.

Manikaran, Himachal now Uttaranchal

We went to Manali with my parents by car, and on our way back took a detour to visit Manikaran Sahib, where there is a Gurdwara where langar or Prasad is served all the time, it is built very near a place where there are hot Sulphur springs! And the rice is cooked from the hot springs steam! It is amazing to see in such a cold place such a wonder of nature! In the middle of the mountains.The place is sacred to the Sikhs as it is believed that Guru Nanak dev jee had come here during one of his Udasis (travels) along with his Muslim disciple, Mardana, who used to accompany him. Apparently Mardana was feeling hungry and though he had been given atta(flour) by the people but there was no fire to cook, Guruji then asked Mardana to pick up a stone, and beneath that there was a hot spring. Mardana put the rolled-up dough in the spring to make rotis but they sank, when he informed Guruji, Guruji said pray to God saying if the rotis float back, I will give one roti as charity. The rotis came back after he prayed.

Kazakhstan

My profile picture on WhatsApp intrigued many people. There is a story behind that picture, where I am seen posing with my arms extended and on one hand an Eagle is sitting with her wings wide, ready to soar. Well it happened like this, my mother-in-law was turning 80 and so the family wanted to celebrate the occasion with something special. Her son and daughter (my wife) found out she preferred an outing with close family over a big party with friends. Her birthday falls on the last day of July. Various destinations were discussed and finally it was decided, the parameters which were to be kept in mind were the following:

1. It should be a new place.
2. It should not be very far, not more than four or five hours by air.
3. The weather should be good, neither too hot or too cold.

Keeping the above in mind, Almaty was ideal! It met all the criteria. Almaty is in Kazakhstan. We all got down to the nitty gritties! Air tickets, Visa, Hotel and Transport arrangements.The close family consisted of the following:

The VIP Birthday girl, her daughter and son in law(myself), Her Son, daughter in law and two children, Our daughter and son in law. Now all the people as mentioned above lived in Delhi except for four that is, son and family who are settled in Vietnam. Anyway, between my son in law and my brother-in-law, all the ends were tied up and we were all set. We all were to travel together from Delhi by Kazakhstan Airlines on the direct Flight. We reached comfortably and on arrival there was a van waiting to take us to the Five Star Hotel which had been booked. The beauty of the van was that all nine of us and of course the driver could be together during our excursions.We had the itinerary planned, we had three full days and we made full use of them.

The place where my profile picture is taken was at the big Almaty Lake, a source of fresh water for Almaty, surrounded by snow clad hills! It is a beautiful place! And there we found ourselves quite the centre of attraction. The locals who had come to sight see the lake on that particular day had not seen creatures like us! We were fellow humans no doubt, but they had not met Sikhs, and I stood out with my red crimson turban! There was some walking and climbing to be done and one lady asked me if she could have a picture clicked with me! I was happy to oblige! Seeing her success, others also seized the opportunity, and I was like a celebrity! Well along the way was this guy holding this beautiful, magnificent bird and was in the business of creating memories for people in exchange for money. He was doing great business and all of us posed seeing that we would perhaps not be visiting Almaty again. This my friends is the story of the profile picture on my What"s App. Hope you liked it. There were other adventures and memories associated with this trip. Perhaps I would write about them another day.

Vietnam

My wife"s, brother had moved to Vietnam some years ago and though Preeti had visited him, Arshiya, my daughter and me, had not been. One day we decided on traveling and applied for visa. Arshiya and myself applied from the embassy here in New Delhi while Jeetan, Preeti"s brother arranged for her Visa on arrival. Our itinerary was Delhi to Bangkok and then onwards a flight on Vietnam Airlines from Bangkok to Ho chi Minh city. We arrived in Bangkok without any issues and stood in the queue for checking in for the final leg of our flight. To our surprise the check in agent said Preeti can board but both of you cannot until we get a message for the Vietnamese Authorities. Anyway, we decided that let Preeti travel while we two would wait, there was another flight after two hours or so. Meanwhile Preeti had already told Jeetan of the problem we were facing. Arshiya and me were in the transit area and spent our time looking around the shops. Fortunately, Jeetan had managed to get a message sent by the Vietnamese Authorities and we were informed that the issue was resolved, and we would be accepted on the next flight. We arrived at Ho chi Minh later than expected after this slight fiasco! Vietnam was quite like India, though under communist rule, it appeared quite relaxed and liberal. The roads at that time, this is about 10 years ago were quite like the roads in India. Crowded and a little rough and bumpy! We enjoyed the hospitality of Jeetan, Simran and her two young children.

Simran cooks and bakes very well and we enjoyed the treats we got at mealtimes and in between. Jeetan suggested to me that one thing that you must do here is to get a massage done. I had never indulged in this luxury in my life! Preeti also acquiesced her consent said 'Yes, you must get it, I had also got one last time.' He dropped me off and explained to the lady in charge there and said we will pick you up after an hour. I was told to go upstairs and take of all my clothes and wrap myself in a towel. Then this young girl with a flawless complexion asked me to lie down on the bed on my stomach. She rubbed oil all over my body and then with her firm hands did her job. It was most enjoyable. Very nice and pleasurable thoughts and feelings were going on in my mind, I did not know her language and she did not know mine. The touch of a feminine hand on my body and getting massaged, felt good. The hour was over, it seemed in a few minutes. They came to pick me up and asked, ' How was it'." Very enjoyable, I said!" I noticed in Vietnam, like in many other South Asian countries, the ladies work much harder, and apparently unlike India where everyone mostly wants a boy, in Vietnam all families welcome the arrival of a girl more than a boy! Ladies work everywhere including at a butcher shop, at every shop we saw mostly women. Today I believe Vietnam Economy is one of the fastest growing and Arshiya, who travelled recently with her husband, told me the change within the last 10 years has been phenomenal! The infrastructure, buildings and roads are most modern. It seems it is time for me to visit Vietnam once more.

Sri Lanka

We thought we will plan something special for our Anniversary. Preeti and me travelled on our Anniversary day, 13 July, from Delhi to Colombo by Air India and since I was now senior enough and as seats were available in Business class, we were upgraded. We had planned our four-day Itinerary through a travel agent in Delhi and everything for the package had been paid in advance.There was a person standing holding my name on a placard as we exited the Airport, and he was our driver cum guide for the duration of our stay. He spoke English quite well and took us straight to Kandy a good 4 hour drive. It was already late evening by the time we reached our hotel. We had just about unpacked in the beautiful room, when there was a knock and on opening the door, the person had a cake in his hands, with Happy Anniversary written on it! We were thrilled! Apparently, our guide from our conversation had learnt it was our Anniversary and planned this little surprise. Kandy was beautiful, it is very hilly and picturesque, we visited the famous Tooth Temple in Kandy which has the tooth of Lord Buddha. Then we drove to Bentota beach and on the way stopped at a herbal and spice garden. There we could see all kinds of spice trees. Pepper, Cardamom, Cloves and so many more. The property where we were put up was a fabulous property, a five-star resort by the beach! We had arrived late and had a plentiful dinner buffet and the next morning enjoyed the beautiful private beach. Then he took us to an Elephant park, we enjoyed the Elephant ride and bathed an elephant! It was a thrilling experience. Next, we went to a tea factory, where so many kinds of tea were displayed and were available for sale too. Sri Lankan tea is famous and amongst the best in the world. We indulged and bought several small cartons of tea, both for gifting and for our own consumption. The turtle farm was next, we were able to pick up turtles in our hands and take lots of pictures. The next stop was Colombo and since we had not stopped while landing, we did some sightseeing and spent the last night in the hotel. We really enjoyed our holiday and do plan to visit again. Sri Lanka derives a lot of income from tourism and as such the Sri Lankans realize this and are very welcoming. Another attraction is that the Indian Rupee is easily acceptable.

Belgium and Paris

My friend was posted as the Ambassador of India at Brussels, Belgium and we thought it is a great opportunity to go there for a short vacation. We, Arshiya, Preeti and me arrived in Frankfurt and booked ourselves in the TGV a fast train which would take us to Brussels. On the way, the train unexpectedly stopped, and we were informed that there is some problem, and the rest of the journey would have to be completed by bus. Luckily, we took the help of a co passenger who had a local phone and informed Ambassador Puri of the situation we were in and that we were likely to arrive quite late. We reached Brussels around midnight instead of 9pm as expected. My friend was waiting for us as we stepped out of the bus. We quickly put our bags, in the boot of the back Mercedes car. We reached India House after a longish 45-minute journey and Namrita, the Ambassador"s wife received us. When the driver brought in the bags, we noticed one bag was missing! And that bag contained among other things, our passports too! It was a panic filled moment and then my friend suggested, why don't you go with the driver to see if it has been left behind where we had disembarked from the bus. I didn't have many hopes and I'm sure, the driver must have been cursing me. The driver took me back and on arrival we saw lots of police people who had cordoned off the area. They were tough looking men equipped with weapons. My bag was lying in the middle and I told them it had got left behind due to an oversight in the excitement our arrival and on meeting my friend. The officer told us, that they were just about to call the bomb squad. I apologized profusely and they were kind enough to give me the bag after verification. I breathed a huge sigh of relief. We were treated so royally, and I compared India House to a Palace. It had a swimming pool and a tennis court too, besides sprawling lawns! We went to Antwerp which is about an hour's drive and had lunch with my school friend, Rajiv Rakyan, a diamond merchant who showed us around his office. He also showed us a person cutting a diamond and he placed a diamond on my wife's finger and said, this cost almost 20000 Dollars or some such exorbitant figure! I promptly clicked a picture of my wife with the stone! Later he hosted us for a vegetarian lunch as he is a pure vegetarian. In the afternoon we went to Waterloo the historic spot where Napoleon was defeated. For Brussels sightseeing Namrita accompanied us and asked me a question, do you know what is the symbol of Brussels? I didn't have a clue, but she said try to guess, and when I couldn't she said I will show it to you. It is called Mannikin pis or the statue of a small boy urinating. It is said that this boy saw a fuse burning and to blow it out, he urinated on it! There's a small statue built depicting the boy and a steam of water flows through his penis! Lots of people get photographs taken there and so did we! We enjoyed the delicious waffles while we were strolling on the streets of Brussels. There are beautiful historical palaces in the city. We bade farewell to Belgium and travelled by bus to Paris where we had booked a hotel very near the centre of Paris, within walking distance of the Eiffel Tower and Arc de Triumph. We had a lot of difficulty in getting a taxi in Paris after getting off the bus. Finally, we took a Metro which dropped us within walking distance from our hotel. We contacted a close friend relative and it was quite late at night, we were tired too, but he said we are in the lobby of your hotel and thought we will show you Paris by night. Padamjee and Madhu, his daughter, then showed us around the city. It was a memorable experience! We saw the beautiful view of Paris at night from the highest point of the city on top of a hill.

Meghalaya

It was the month of February and we decided to visit Shillong and celebrate my birthday. We flew to Guwahati and had arranged a car to drive us to the place we had booked for our stay. We had booked a cottage through some friends and had also taken a package whereby they would show us the sights. It was a long journey by road from Guwahati to Shillong. It took close to three and a half hour to reach. Our cottage was beautiful, and we had a lovely fireplace which the young boys who were our guides lit for us. We ordered a simple meal and slept. The next morning, they took us to the cleanest village in the country and we visited the famous root Bridge. A bridge entirely made from the roots of a tree. The cleanest village located in the east Khasi hills is called Mawlynnong. On the way we stopped at a place where they had a zip line. I had never done this, so I opted to do the easier and cheaper trip. It was enjoyable but later I felt I should have opted for the longer and more expensive and spectacular crossing between the two mountains. But I guess I was scared a little! We went to see the border between India and Bangladesh too and saw hundreds of trucks carrying coal, which our guides told us, was being sold at much higher price illegally. The best part of our trip was the visit to a lake which was so clean, we could see through the water! Then we took a boat ride on it and reached near a small waterfall and had a lovely lunch by the riverside. The next day was 17th February and my birthday, and we had planned to travel back to Delhi. Just on a hunch I asked, isn't there a helicopter service between Shillong and Guwahati and the boys said, 'yes there is.' We went to the helicopter booking office and checked if there was a service and what was the cost. It was very reasonable and suited us and would take only 20 minutes or so. We thought let's go for it, as we had never had a helicopter ride. It was a thrilling experience and an apt way to celebrate my birthday! There are many more memories of my travels in India and Abroad, but due to space limitations, I cannot relate them. I will end by writing two quotes very apt for Never Ending Footsteps.

"Wandering one gathers honey!"

And

"A rolling stone gathers no moss!"

Life itself is a journey, enjoy it. Travel wide and far, discover new places and discover yourself too! We have only one life, live it fully while you still can! Hope you enjoyed reading about my travels. And travails!

Change

Let me say one thing. I am going to talk about the changes I have seen myself! I am already 64 so I have seen a few, no many! I was born in 1959 in Delhi in a middle-class family. We lived in a government flat as my father was in the government service. In my early days, we were comfortable and happy, we lived a decent simple life, the pace of life was slow, everyone had time for one another. We knew our neighbours. There was very little crime. In summers we slept on the terrace. There was no TV, no air conditioners, the roads were not crowded and there were much fewer cars. We used to drink water, straight from the tap. There was no cassette player or computer. I am talking about the sixties. No computer and no internet, and of course no mobile phone! There were only two models of cars. Ambassador and Fiat. Maruti came much later! No car had A/C! As time passed, changes happened slowly at first, then as time moved on, the changes grew rapidly! TV came, black and white, only one channel, movie shown in parts, over two days! TV was a big thing! The TV owner would let in a lot of friends and children would sit on the floor and watch!! In 1982 came colour TV and just before the start of Asiad 82... the time of the Asian Games, people were crazy to buy colour TV! they went abroad, paid duty and proudly displayed their Sony TV. The VCR came, the cassette player had already arrived. The Maruti car made an appearance in the early eighties. And in a few years, the roads were full of Maruti cars, and the fiats and Ambassadors were hardly to be seen. As the years pass so many changes took place, in every sphere, in every field, in how one dressed how one spoke, what one ate, there were many choices available. In fact, I used to hear, as a small boy, that in Europe people bought water to drink. I was amazed, people buying water!! Why? it is available free, it comes in the tap! And now, in India, it is common to buy water. Today we don't get any car without A/C Automatic cars are getting popular, Tomorrow Electric cars will rule, who knows in the future, there will be cars that fly!!

For me, a most amazing moment was; I had gone to London, availing my free passage facility as I worked in air India, and there, I was flabbergasted to see in 1985, someone talking on a phone without wires, I just couldn't accept it! The changes in Mobile phones too have been phenomenal, at first the phone was big, heavy and bulky, the call rates were very high! And there were no smart phones. Today one can't exist without a smart phone, it works like a camera, a computer, like an office, you can do your bank transactions, you can buy anything you want, just at the click of a button! Change is very strange!! And if someone from the past, say a hundred years ago were to come and see our world, well he wouldn't be able to believe his eyes! There is only one thing constant in life and that is change!

Guilt

This happened many years ago, and the feeling of guilt will never go. I was a small boy, maybe 8 years old at the time. We had a new help in the house, a servant, for want of a better word. My Father had just bought for me a new badminton racquet and I had gone happily to play with my friend at his house. It so happened, the racquet broke, it was perhaps only a few days old. I was shattered and didn't have the courage to tell my father the truth, perhaps I feared a scolding or even worse. I told my father; the servant broke it. My Father called the servant and questioned him, and he obviously said, he had nothing to do with it. My father felt he was lying as he trusted me more than him. The result, the poor guy was turned out. My parents felt, he could not be trusted. This guilt of having harmed an innocent poor person will stay with me forever. I have not shared this with anyone.

Flying Kites

I was a little boy, around 6 or 7 years old. My brother was 5 years older than me and he used to fly kites. I am talking of the time in Delhi in the mid-sixties. So, we would go to the terrace and he used to ask me to do kanni! Which means I had to go some distance and hold the kite, and he would pull the string and hoist the kite, up in the sky. Now I used to watch, while he used to enjoy flying the patang. I too wanted to fly but he would hardly let me, sometimes he would allow me to hold the string, but that was not enough for me. I wanted to fly the kite myself. One day I had not gone to school and was alone in the house, I found 10 rupees in my father's drawer and I thought, this is a good chance to buy some kites and enjoy. I went to the corner where the kite seller sat on the pavement and got some kites, chadkhadi (wooden device with handles on which string is wrapped) and Saddi. (string) The man gave me a lot of change back, and I happily went home and went to the terrace. I put the string on the kite, like I had seen my brother do. And I flew the kite!! All on my own. I was thrilled at my achievement! Then I really enjoyed myself for about an hour or so!! I was very happy!! In the evening my father came and said, I had kept a 10 rupee note in the drawer, but it's not there now. And my brother went to the kite guy and he told him, your brother had come and bought kites. So, my father questioned me, I was scared but he was very nice. He didn't beat me but rather explained to me that what I did was not right. But I felt very ashamed! And my brother used to keep taunting me..for many years for stealing 10 rupees! I hated that. This was one demon; I overcame in later years!

Unsaid Feelings

What should I write about my unsaid feelings, or thoughts. So many times, I didn't say it out loud, at times it was for the best. At times it would have been better if they were expressed. We are bound by rules and regulations, some societal norms, it is not always prudent to speak out what you feel. There are feelings of love, of passion, of hate, of irritation, of regret, of sorrow, of sympathy and boredom amongst so many other feelings. There are pure feelings and impure feelings. The feelings one gets actually define the person that you are. I just wish we were less hypocrites; we show something but feel something else. In this respect babies are so pure, they express their feelings, if they are angry, content, hungry or hurt they express it immediately. Pets are also like that absolutely pure souls. We get know their feelings instantly! The feelings which trouble me most are, I wish I had not done that, I wish I had not committed so many sins, wish I had not hurt some people, wish I could have been a better person, I wish I could have fulfilled my potential.

The Drowning

We were friends, Jasvir and me. We were from the same school, Modern School, and the incident I relate happened many years ago. I was in Shri Ram College in the second year of economics honours and Jasvir had just secured admission in medical college, the prestigious All India Institute of Medical Studies. The year was 1978 or 1979, so more than forty years ago! Jasvir and me weren't all that friendly in school but became quite close later, he lived in Defence Colony whereas I was in South Extension. After school he joined Hindu College and at times, he used to give my sister a lift as she was doing MA at Delhi School of Economics which was just adjacent to Hindu College. In those days we started meeting almost daily. I would be at their house often. Jasvir was a slightly built boy and quite eccentric, he was very intelligent as only the brightest get admission to All India Institute of Medical Science AIIMS He introduced me to several new things, including my first alcoholic drink! And also, I saw a Squash Court for the first time in my life. I hadn't heard about Squash, so, when Jasvir suggested "Let's play Squash", I was curious and we went to IIT in his old white Standard Herald! Anyway, enough of the background! So, one day he suggested "Let's go swimming", and I said, "but I don't know how to swim". It's very easy, he said. So, for the next couple of days, we went to the Aiims swimming pool, which was an Olympic sized open-air pool. Since I didn't know swimming, I used to practise on the shallow side of the pool. Jasvir used to guide and encourage me, so on the third day we went swimming again. I went on my Bajaj 150 Scooter to pick him up from B-45 Defence Colony. This time Jasvir told me, "Why don't you try swimming in the deep". I told him "Don't be silly, I don't know swimming, I will drown." He said "Don't worry, I'm there, besides you've already picked up and it's much easier to swim in the deep". Much against my will and my good sense, I got persuaded and reached the deep end by clinging to the wall. Then I tried to swim and my head didn't come up and I wasn't able to. But since I knew Jasvir was there I didn't really panic, actually I did panic as I wasn't able to swim but I thought he is there so he will save me from drowning. But nothing happened I used to go down as I was almost vertical and then due to the buoyancy of the water, I used to come up a bit then again go down. All the time my head was in the water and I couldn't breathe. I had the good sense not to take in any water from my mouth and this torture went on for a few minutes, it was quite a terrible feeling and then I must have blacked out. The next thing that I know was that I was by the side of the pool and I had a big smile on my face. There were people looking at me, I was on my stomach and an elderly gentleman was pressing my back. Jasvir was there too and he was in a little bit of a shock. He told me, imagine my plight, what would I have told people! Anyway, I was quite alright and I got up and asked him what had happened, " who pulled me out, why didn't you save me I asked". He said he tried but couldn't manage and was scared if I held his hand he would drown too. Luckily someone searched for the swimming coach whom I hadn't seen before. The person who was pressing my back was the coach. He was an elderly person, maybe in his fifties with grey hair and was stocky. Apparently, he was an ex-Army man. So, he had saved my life. Apparently, I was in the water for quite a few minutes and had been fished out by the coach with the help of a pole. Jasvir said my body had become all blue. I was quite alright by now and I thanked the coach and I drove my scooter as normal and dropped Jasvir off and went home. It had been a traumatic morning; I think it was a Saturday or a Sunday and I was home by afternoon. That day I didn't tell anyone about the incident at home. Jasvir told me that the person who saved your life, you must at least give him an adequate reward. So the next day I told my parents what had happened and I recall we decided to make a basket of fruits and Jasvir and me went and gave it to him. In conclusion, I would say, Life is not in our hands, the same goes for death!

I had almost gone. Then God... In the form of the coach, who wasn't even around when I was in the pool, pulled me out! We should be sensible of course; I shouldn't have done what I did. Also, Jasvir was lucky I lived that day! Would have been traumatic for him. Unfortunately, Jasvir passed away in a small plane that he was piloting himself, some months ago, along with his wife and one daughter. He is survived by another daughter and his parents. This happened in the United States of America. I lost touch with Jasvir and all of us were shocked at getting this sad news.

Table Tennis

As I look back at this long and beautiful journey, my mind gets filled up with pleasant and plenty of memories. I first saw a TT Table when we were living in Chanakya Puri. A colony for Government Servants located in South Delhi. I must have been around 6 years old then, the year 1966 or thereabouts. There was a Naval club nearby and our parents took us there to have a look. We saw people playing badminton and Table Tennis. Now my brother, who was 5 years older than me started going regularly to play table tennis and I would accompany him. However, since I was small, they did not give me a chance to play. I really wanted to play too, it was quite fascinating to watch, to hear the sound of the ball going tuk... Tuk.on the table. And two players hitting the ball, and while doing so, again the bat making a sound upon touching the ball! Well, I did not get a chance to play in the hall, but what I did, I started hitting the ball in my house against the wall, so I would hit it on the wall, wait for it to fall on the ground and then again hit against the wall. It was better than not being able to play and with practice I was able to do some long rallies. I could control the ball better with each day's practice and knew when to hit hard or softer so that the ball came back to me. Sometimes I would just hit the ball with the bat gently and wait for it to come down to the bat again without falling on the ground, so tap, tap, tap, tap I would practice how many times I could keep the ball in my control without it falling to the ground.

Now a magical thing happened, the year was 1968 I think, my father got a posting at Kathmandu and decided to take the whole family along except my brother who was in a senior class so that his studies would not get affected. At Kathmandu the place where we were staying was called Hari Bhawan. It was the erstwhile Palace of the father of the Queen of Nepal, which had been converted into the office of the Indian Cooperation Mission, this Palace had a few Residences as well. And while surveying the building I discovered a room where there was a table and middle-aged Nepali men used to play, some of them with pretty big bellies used to play with their shirts off, in their vests. I used to watch them play. I wanted to play too, and sometimes they would oblige. There was another development as well which really benefited me. A South Indian family moved in and were staying at the guest house, also in Hari Bhawan. And their eldest son Arvind was my age. They had moved in from Bombay or Madras, I'm not really sure and I found out that Arvind played Table Tennis too! Well then, we both started playing, he had played earlier and was good at it. While he was an attacking player;

I was more defensive. And the good thing was that we had the table to ourselves as the elder guys would come only later after office finished. Sometimes he would win and sometimes me, it was great fun! And that's how my journey with table tennis started. In Nepal we used to get a lot of Chinese goods too and I got a good TT bat, Double Happiness was the brand name. I remember after my father's posting got over, I packed my TT racquet carefully and it came with the other household goods in a truck after many days. In Kathmandu, in my school St Xavier's there was a TT table too, but there was only one table and not enough time to play. I remember one of our teachers, a very handsome Kingsley Sir, who used to teach us English and was the most popular teacher, was very good at Tt. We could not pick up his services, he was that good! Well Arvind shifted out of the guest house but his new house was not too far off and we continued playing when we could. Thereafter Arvind shifted to a more distant place called Swarna Bhawan and that place had a table too. There were a lot of officers of ICM staying at Swarna Bhawan and whenever we used to go there, we would play. Arvind became my best friend. His sister Kanchana and my younger sister Manjula were also the best of friends.

Another Sikh family moved into Satya Bhawan which was adjacent to Swarna Bhawan and this place had a table too. Our parents used to visit this family at times and I made friends with

Harbir. Now Arvind, Harbir and me became good friends. Arvind unfortunately is no longer with us, he passed away many years ago in Chennai. Harbir is settled in USA and was a very good badminton player, he Captained the Delhi University badminton team in his time. Well in 1971, my father was transferred back to Delhi. We stayed with my uncle at Jangpura Extension for a while till my father got government accommodation. Here as luck would have it, my cousin who used to live nearby had a table and I remember though he was about 7 years elder than me, I could compete well with him.

My father got accommodation in East Kidwai Nagar, and I got admitted to Air Force Central School. I was in the 7th class. I saw that they were planning on trials for the table tennis team and I gave my name for the trials. I remember I played quite well and would have got selected but for an unfortunate incident. My parents suddenly told me that they were planning to shift me to Modern School. I was very upset as I had adjusted now to this school, made friends and was likely to make the school table tennis team. But what could I do, I was compelled to go to the new school. The advantage of Modern School was that they encouraged sports and there were a number of games played there including table tennis. During the school break times we would run up to the area where the TT table was and we used to enjoy playing. Around the same time, my father got better accommodation and shifted to Multi Storeyed Flats in R. K. Puram. By a stroke of good fortune Arvind's father also got transferred to Delhi and they were staying in Moti Bagh, which was nearby. One could even walk to his place. We used to meet every evening and play cricket or just hang out together. We both had bicycles and we found out that there is a Community Hall in nearby Nanak Pura where they had a TT table. We went to see it and found out the formalities of playing there. There were slots of an hour each and the prime slots were already full. We got a slot of 5 to 6 am, early morning and our love for the game was so much that we took up that slot, of course after permission from our parents. I used to go on my cycle ring his bell and we used to play for an hour, come back and go to our respective schools. We both were so fond of the game that we played in the winter too!

Life was beautiful, one day, what happened, we saw a notice at the community hall that a table tennis tournament was being organized at the community hall, there was an entry fee and we could participate in two categories, men's and boy's". Arvind and me both participated and I won the boys title after a thrilling match with a slightly built sardar boy called Little! Arvind was the runners up in the Men's category. We both got small trophies, my first ever prize I won at Table Tennis. The person who gave us the prizes was Mr Thiruvengadam who used to stay in Nanakpura. He was at one time the coach of the

Indian National team. Around the same time, since both of us had arrived in a way, we took part in our first big tournament. It was the Times of India Table - Tennis open, and we entered our names in the boys" category. Both of us played well and to our pleasant surprise, on the sports page of T. O. I Arvind made the headline as he had lost narrowly to a seeded player. I too did well and lost narrowly to another seeded player, making him sweat a lot! In the mean while I got selected in my school table tennis team, Mr Thiruvengadam used to occasionally come to our school to impart coaching. In between one day my prized possession, the racquet I had got from Nepal, got stolen from my school bag. I was shocked and made a big noise about it, complained to the vice principal too. I think because of the announcement in the assembly too, the person who had taken it must have chickened out and the racquet was found!

I got a firing from the vice principal too, "Why do you get such an expensive thing to school". Well, we took part in other tournaments, in interschool matches but I was never at the top, I was above average but I enjoyed playing. Arvind's father got transferred to Chennai and I lost touch with him. Years later I had met him when I went after my college for an interview to Bangalore, SSB Service Selection Board, for getting into the Army. I had qualified the written paper, but ultimately didn't get selected. They had given me a train ticket for the journey and on the return, there was a six-hour halt of the train at Madras. So, I had been able to contact Arvind and he came to meet me at the Railway Station. We went around a bit, including to Marina beach I recall. It was great meeting him. Unfortunately, a few months after that, my parents conveyed to me the news that he had passed away. Apparently, he fell out from the window of his house which was on a high floor. It was a shock to me! He was a close friend, we had spent a lot of time together, playing, cycling and seeing movies. Well, I played some tournaments and played with some good players, some of whom represented India too. I mostly lost to these good players but it was a pleasure playing with them. A few times I beat some good players so that was a big achievement for me.

One highlight I would like to share. It so happened that per chance I had gone to Nanakpura and Mr Thiru met me and said that trials are going on for selection for the Delhi schools" team, to represent Delhi in the National Schools games. This was in 1974. Nobody had told me about this and the trials were being held in my school itself. I went there and several players were there, mostly from Delhi Public School who had beaten us and had won the Inter School championship. My school captain was also, there. The organizer decided to conduct league matches, in which everyone plays with everyone and then they select the best 6 for the team. I played well and defeated my captain too.

Eventually I was selected and we went to Agra. I was not in the playing team as the players from DPS were better. But it was a good experience. We were given a badge and a certificate and I was proud, I got a Blazer stitched, I and the badge could be attached on the coat pocket, which said Delhi Table Tennis 1974 National School Games, Agra, Autumn meet! Subsequently I was awarded the school colours too at a ceremony in which several others were honoured too. The colours were given by the then Vice President of India, Shri B. D. Jatti who was the chief guest for the day. I wasn't aware that I was being awarded and per chance I happened to be around and a friend told me, better dress up properly, you are going to be awarded. Apparently, it was a last moment decision to award all those who had represented Delhi. I borrowed the school blazer from a friend in the hostel and received the award. Thereafter I made the college team too. Then the Air India team. We got married in 1986 and it so happened that a few months after that there was an Airlines SAARC Table tennis tournament being held at Kathmandu, Nepal. I was selected to be a member of the Air India team and I took my wife too along with me. It was great going to Kathmandu after all these years and after the matches, my wife and me managed to spend some time together. Another interesting thing happened during the 1982 Asian Games held in Delhi. I was out of college and looking for a job and I got the opportunity to work for the games as a Guide in the Protocol Section and was also selected later as a Technical Official Grade A, Announcer, Badminton. Now while in the protocol section, we were making Identity cards for the officials and it so happened that I made friends with two Japanese Table tennis umpires and also invited them home. They even gifted me a table tennis bat! But the highlight was that, it just happened by chance that I happened to be outside the Hall of Nations, where the Finals of the Table Tennis championship match had just got over between China and Japan. China won quite easily. Mr Mawatari, one of the Japanese Umpires, saw me and gestured to me to get into the car with him. There were other cars too and we all went to Hotel Vikram and had something to eat there. The entire Japanese team, both Women and Men were there and we were seated together. It was awesome. In those days we didn't have mobile phones, else I would have clicked a picture with them! However, they were all talking in Japanese and I couldn't understand a thing. Amongst the players was also a former World Champion. Mr Mawatari told me you are very lucky to be in this gathering and he suggested I could take their autographs! So, we found a large piece of paper and all of them obliged, but all signatures were in Japanese language! Mr Mawatari then wrote below them in English their names! I had got this prized possession framed too! Years later in 1991 or so, I travelled to Tokyo on a short vacation and was able to talk to both the gentlemen. Mr Mawatari spoke broken English and was very happy, he wanted me to go and meet him. But he was in Osaka and I was in Tokyo and I didn't go because of the logistics. I continue to play TT and some of my best friends have been made thanks to this game. We played on weekends or holidays as on other days we had office to attend to. Once a year we play in the school, a sports event is organized by MSOSA, Modern School old students Association. It is very well conducted and various games are played between the school team and the ex-students like us called Mordenites" all are given T Shirts and refreshments and it is a joy to meet up with school mates and to visit the school and play with the school children. These days, I am missing playing due to the COVID-19 threat. Since I am diabetic and 61, it is safer to avoid playing at the moment. When things get better, I plan to start again!! A big lesson from the game is that it starts with " Love all" Also it has everything in it, skill, luck, exercise, it can be played in all kinds of weather as it is an indoor game. It teaches us hand eye coordination, improves our reflexes, above all anyone can play it! It is enjoyable and relaxing!! It teaches us how to win and how to lose too with grace. Thank you for your time! I love this game, so I wanted to write it.

The Accident - Bajaj 150

This happened many years ago. We were in Delhi; the capital city of India and it was summer time in the evening. The year was 1978, I think. I was in second year of college, and that year I didn't pass the second-year exam, perhaps the accident came in handy. To blame! It happened like this, a year or so earlier I had been gifted a scooter, Bajaj 150, I still remember the registration number, DHJ-7815. Well, the condition for getting this gift was that "in case we ask you to do some errands you have to agree to do them" to which I had readily agreed. Now at that time I had adopted a routine of playing badminton in the nearby community hall at Andrew's Ganj where we were staying. This hall was about a five-minute drive by the scooter from our residence. And just as I was ready to go to play, my mother told me to pick up my father from his office at RK Puram, which was about seven to eight kilometres from our house. I was upset, as it was my time to play, and I used to look forward to it! Normally my father used to come back from office independently. He used to drive down in our car, so this was unexpected. But anyway because of my promise, I had to go. I drove very fast on the ring road and reached my father's office, only to find that he wasn't there. I was so angry!! I had been specially sent to pick him up and he wasn't there. So, in a very angry mood I started back. On the way I thought, since I am nearby, why don't I stop by to pick up a record from my friend who was staying nearby my father's office in the Multi Storeyed flats at Sector 13. Listening to music was my passion and so quickly I went to Rahul's house and he lent me the "Carpenters Album Singles" I think it was. So now I thought I can still make it to play at Andrew's Ganj, I needed to just pick up my racquet from home. So, in order to reach on time, I drove very fast on ring road. The playing time at the hall was limited, as our booking was for one hour only at the daily fixed time from 5 to 6pm. It was already 530. So, I thought I could still make it if I drove fast. So, I revved up the accelerator and was driving at about 80 km per hour speed.I was approaching the AIIMS crossing when suddenly I saw a fiat car turning from the other side of the road. The gentleman driving was apparently returning home to West Kidwai Nagar after office. He should have seen before he turned into the cut. However, he perhaps did not see me, or my speed was very high, I can't say. I had only a split second between my seeing the car and my scooter hitting the car, full side on. There was nothing I could do. It was a terrifying split second. Then Bang!! I had hit the car head on! The front part of the scooter, the front wheel must have been the first one to have hit the car. And I must have flown off and my face hit the side of the car. I was on the ground and in pain. Luckily my head did not hit the car as my arms must have instinctively gone forward to protect myself, else I would have died on the spot. At that speed a head injury would have been fatal on a two-wheeler and since I was a Sardar, I was in a turban, no helmet. The scooter was on the ground too, the front part twisted and the record which I had kept in the front rack on the scooter had broken, a big crack in it! I was spitting out teeth. The crowd gathered. They saw the situation. By God's grace, I had not lost consciousness. Someone asked my address and so I was able to tell my address and phone number. The crowd put me in the same car I had hit. Of course, all this time I was in a lot of pain and was groaning and moaning in pain, spurting out blood and fragments of broken teeth. And the guy with whom I had the accident told me, don't worry, nothing has happened, and took me to Safdarjung Hospital which was just across the road. From there he must have called up my parents to tell them that I had a minor accident and there was nothing to worry. Since many years now thankfully they have blocked that cut. There may have been more accidents like mine.

Well, the doctors at the emergency started doing their thing. What could I do, I was pretty helpless. Now not known to me, I came to know this later! A good Samaritan, a young Sardar jee, part of the crowd which had gathered, must have heard me speak out my address and phone number. He was so sweet, I have never met him or seen him, but he drove in his bicycle to my parents" house. They had already been informed by this South Indian elderly gentleman with whom I had the accident, that it is a minor accident, he should be discharged soon and nothing to worry. So, they were not too worried, I guess. However, when this boy told my parents that it was a bad accident and your son has been injured quite a bit, they rushed to the hospital to be with me. I remember my father taking notes in a small diary about my injuries and dos and don'ts. He was very meticulous and his handwriting was beautiful. I was trying to locate that diary so that I could give a more authentic account of the injuries and dos and don'ts, but I couldn't find it. Many teeth had been broken, around 10 in all, five upper and five lowers. All the teeth were the ones which are most visible in a smile! The impact had been so hard that it was found out that one tooth had broken into three fragments and was Imbedded in the upper gums. Later these fragments had to be removed surgically. My collar bone was fractured. My right wrist too had a fracture if I recall. But the worst was my mouth area. My mouth had swollen up so much!! It was quite like a chimpanzee! The jaw had been fractured in a few places and there was a rather deep cut just above my right eye. Some minor bruises on both knees. They shifted me to the Burns and plastic surgeries ward. I was not allowed to eat or drink with my mouth for fear of infection and I was fed through a Ryle"s tube. A small tube which is inserted through the nose. I remember it was very painful while they tried to shove it in. All the while I remember my mother say "Bahut bachav ho gaya". He is fortunate, things could have been much worse. I remember telling my parents to sue the guy with the fiat, but they didn't consider that at all, they were just thankful that their son was alive. I still felt that they should have sued him or taken compensation from him, I was badly hurt, the scooter was damaged and my treatment would cost a lot of money.

In fact, even years after my accident I have had to go to the dentist regularly as first they made dentures, then caps for the teeth, but the caps would come off as there was not much support for them. Till date I am not comfortable with my dentures and I take them off when I eat. At home I dislike wearing the dentures, I only wear them when I need to go out. Because of the above I felt the person should have been sued. But what to do, it didn't happen that way. Well, I was admitted to the burns ward after they had done the figure of eight bandage for my collar bone, wired up the jaw and other stuff which they needed to do. For ten uncomfortable days and nights I was in the hospital. My roommate was a middle-aged man who was very cheerful and had a big hole in the neck and was fed by a funnel through that hole. I was amazed at his demeanour. How come a person in such a state of health be happy, I used to wonder. Anyway, my mother decided that one of my uncles would spend the night. During the day my parents and I am sure my sisters too came to visit. I felt such a relief when the tube was finally pulled out from my nose and I could taste something from the mouth! Before that they would allow a couple of spoons of water only or some juice or coconut water through the mouth. It was tough to stay on the hospital bed for a young man like me. Due to no exercise, I also put on a lot of weight. I used to long to walk but the hospital guys wouldn't allow. Then at night I would plead with my uncle and convince him and step out of the room for a walk. So that was the story of the accident. In the meantime I was concerned about the scooter too and was told people from my father's office have taken it for repair. My parents asked me what to do with it. They asked should we give it away or sell it. I however, was adamant to keep it. It had given me a lot of independence.

Well dear readers I kept that scooter for a long time. I got married in July 1986 and I had the scooter. Then I got posted to Bombay, as it was called then in 1993 and the same scooter was of great use to me. I had it transported by air from Delhi to Bombay. Later on, after coming back to Delhi I was transferred to Ahmedabad and the same scooter gave me good service. I was very proud of that scooter, it was only recently, say five or six years ago that there was another accident on the scooter and my wife took a stand and finally the scooter was given away. So, the scooter was my companion for more than 35 years! More than the time I have been married! Many a times the thought had come to me that what a wonderful piece of machinery Bajaj Auto has made! I thought of writing a nice letter in praise of the scooter to Mr Rahul Bajaj but I never got around to doing that! I hope you enjoyed reading this true story! In conclusion I just want to say, Accidents happen, no one does them on purpose. Two wheelers are vulnerable as the rider does not have any protection unlike a four-wheeler. Also, many a times the fault may not be with the driving of the two-wheeler, but the damage is always more to the two-wheeler and the driver because it will fall down. If you are a two-wheel driver, drive safe, drive slowly! Don't drive fast and rash like I did, in anger!

Thank you for reading this.

My First Job

My parents were very worried. And so was I. I had finished schooling in Delhi and had with great difficulty managed to graduate. But I didn't have good marks. My father was a government servant. An engineer and in our family, there was nobody doing business. My elder brother was in the merchant navy and both my sisters were good at studies. This used to pinch me even more, as I used to compare myself with them. In fact, it used to be hurtful and embarrassing for me when my mother would discuss with relatives or friends" children around my age, saying so and so's daughter is becoming a doctor or someone's son has got into IIT! I would just feel bad, and actually speaking, I had no one to blame but myself! I had never really put in the effort! For that too. I would blame my parents, "why were you not strict with me". It's easy to put the blame for your situation onto someone else! So, I used to tell my parents... "why did you change my school, without asking me?" " I was doing well in the previous school, yet you changed my school, and in this new school there was no discipline, so because of that I didn't study!" Well anyway I managed to get admission to a good college as I had got a first division but I was very upset with my marks, as everyone else in my class in school had done better than me. I chose to do Economics Honours at a college in Delhi. We lived in Delhi, in a place called South Extension. In those days, I'm talking about the year 1976, there used to be a waiting period for everything! Now it so happened that my father had applied to buy a scooter. A two-wheeler about a dozen years ago, that too in my mother's name! And as luck would have it, she got a letter from Bajaj Scooters that "The scooter you had booked is ready for delivery, please pay Rs 4000/..within two weeks or else it will be allotted to the next person in the waiting list." In our family no one had ridden a two-wheeler, except of course a bicycle which I used to ride. My father asked me," would you like to have a scooter?" I was overjoyed! I was just out of school and to have my own scooter!! Wow!! That would be so awesome!! I said Yes!! Then my mother put in the condition, "OK we will get you the scooter, but you must do errands for us when we ask you to" I readily agreed to this. Well perhaps the background is getting a bit long for you dear reader. So, I will hasten up the story! I had the scooter with me, College had started and with it came new found independence! new friends, and a young age with wheels beneath me! It was a heady combination! With liberal parents, I had a great time. Movies, games, buying records! Going out on my scooter to friends" houses!! The time passed nicely. But again, due not applying myself to studying, I didn't do well in college.

I blamed the college lecturers for this, they didn't teach well! All the students in college did badly! It was easy to blame them. I used to say, we used to wait for the teacher to come, as there was a long gap at times between classes and he did not show up, so this was the reason, I lost interest in studies. To cut this short, eventually I graduated but due to poor marks was awarded a pass course degree without division!! I didn't even know that such a thing existed, but apparently if you are doing an honours course and if you get above 33%, they give you a BA pass course degree! So now there was some hope at least. As a graduate I could apply for jobs, could appear for the civil services too. However, some avenues were blocked. I could not do an MBA as they required a minimum of 50% marks in graduation, which I did not have. I had actually cleared the written test for admission to the MBA program at the Faculty of Management Studies, Delhi University. However, I did not go to the interview as I would not have been eligible for admission. The written test for MBA is held before the results for graduation are announced. I could not apply at the Law Faculty at Delhi University for the same reason. They too had a requirement for at least 50% marks at the graduate exam. For a long time since 1981 to 1983, two long years of my life! I was an unemployed graduate. You can well imagine my mental state as well as the anguish my parents would have gone through.

My mother, who was a very social person took me to meet someone she knew at the top level, a Director at Dunlop Company, Dunlop Tyres if I'm not mistaken. I still remember his name, Mr MM Sabharwal, we had gone to his residence. Though he couldn't offer me a job, but he gave me a pep talk, he said he too had not done well in studies, and here he was, a director at a top-level company. He told me, don't lose heart!

During this time, when all my friends were moving ahead in life, I was actually doing nothing. Well almost nothing! I finally felt that now the only thing left is to try for the IAS (The Civil service exam) for which the requirement was that one must be a graduate and must clear the preliminary examination and the main examination and thereafter the interview. I cleared the Preliminary exam which I found to be quite easy, as it was based on general knowledge and current affairs. Then in order to prepare for the Final examination I joined some coaching classes. However, I was not able to study as much as was required. I did not clear the main exam. In the meantime, to pass the time I joined some French Classes, I started playing badminton and also played bridge and billiards at Delhi Gymkhana club where my father was a member. All along I used to look out for job advertisements in the newspapers. But everyone wanted persons with experience. Now my parents were quite worried. What will happen to this boy, they would think?

They took me to meet my uncle who was very respected in our family and was also at one time Chairman of Punjab and Sind Bank for advice. He suggested that why doesn't he try his hand at business. The Construction business he said was a safe business and his own son was into it. So, he suggested make a company, it needs a little investment only and then you can start. He said I will help in giving him a loan.

So, a company called Jagmit Builders and Engineers was formed! I was asked to go to my cousin's construction site and observe how buildings are constructed. I went for a few days and I found the process absolutely BORING! Sitting in the hot sun and watching the laborers putting bricks!! was not my cup of tea! One day, I came across an advertisement. In fact, there were two Ads that I thought I could apply to. One was a job with Johnson and Johnson, they wanted a sales representative, they preferred a science graduate. The other was a sales representative job at Godrej Soaps. I applied for both jobs. As luck would have it I was called for an interview at Johnson and Johnson and even though I was not a science graduate I fared well in the interview. Then there was another interview and finally I was selected! I was elated!! Finally, a job!! That too with a reputed multinational company! Now the only formality left was to clear the medical examination. I still remember the Doctors name, a Sikh gentleman in Kirti Naga Dr Nanra. But there was a shock in store for me. My blood pressure was too high! The doctor too was surprised and then said, I will have to reject you. You can imagine my disappointment! But what could I do. Anyway, I got a call from Godrej soaps as well, and to cut the story short, after group discussion and two interviews, the last one with Mr SP Godrej, I was selected subject to medical? Here again I was rejected on medical grounds for the same reason.

Now coincidentally one of our neighbours, whose daughter was working in Air India pointed out to her dad about an advertisement from Air India seeking interested graduates for the post of Traffic Assistant in the Commercial Department. She too was working as a traffic assistant and her father alerted my parents about the advertisement as we might have missed it, it was a small advertisement.

Now I was quite keen and an Airline job appealed to me especially as I had heard about the free tickets for staff and the opportunity to travel. I was told by the lady that don't worry, you will easily clear the written test as your English and general knowledge is good. I remember appearing for the written test at YMCA Delhi amongst many other candidates. It was an objective type test and quite easy for me. I did very well in it. I cleared the test and was called for an interview. The interview too went well and I was selected, again subject to medical clearance. This time, having been twice bitten I consulted a family friend who was a doctor and told him the background. He suggested that before my medical I should have this tablet and I would be fine. This is what I did. However, the story doesn't end here. Though my blood pressure was OK, I needed to get some blood tests done and report again to the doctor with the results in a sealed envelope from the doctor. And in my case since I was overweight, I was asked to do an extra test, namely, Glucose tolerance test, which requires drinking a lot of glucose and blood being drawn every half an hour for two and a half hours!

So, I still remember this doctor who I thought was obnoxious and intolerant at the time, his name was Dr. Sarin. Now his laboratory was in Connaught place, in one of the inner lanes on the second floor. It so happened that on that particular day there was no electricity and it was peak summer! My mother had brought me for these tests in the car and was accompanying me. I was running out of patience so I told the doctor that I can't stay here in the heat, I will come back but he wouldn't listen. At one point I told my mother, I am not staying here! She got worried too! Actually, the doctor wanted to make sure that I didn't drink any water or eat anything during the course of that time. My mom pleaded with me, thinking in her mind no doubt, at last he is getting a job and look how he is behaving! Well, the test got over, and finally I went with the report to the lady medical doctor. And now the last bit, she was a young lady doctor, couldn't have been much older than me. Perhaps she was on temporary duty with Air India. She asked me to strip, completely!! And cough!! It was a little embarrassing but part of her medical duty I suppose. I later came to know; it was to check if I had hernia. That completed my medical exam and I was told to go home. This is not the end! I then got a letter asking me to join by a particular date else failing which it would be presumed I was not interested in joining. It so happened that I fell unwell, I had fever and had a psychiatric issue too, so my father consulted a doctor and was advised not to send me for joining as I was not in a state and it might be disastrous if I joined then. So, the doctor advised me rest for a month and my father responded to the Air India letter attaching the medical certificate advising me rest. Air India then wrote back saying alright let him join once he gets alright. Subsequently I think I joined a couple of months after my final medical episode with the lady doctor. In between telegrams used to come from the administration department of Air India advising me to join., to which replies would be generated by my father in response.

Finally on 11 July 1983 I joined Air India, my first permanent job! Also, my last permanent job where I served for more than thirty-three years! And that my friends is the true story of my first job. Today as I look back at my life, at my childhood, school, college, and how I got my first and last permanent job, I feel grateful. For a person like me who hadn't put in the required effort at the proper time, life has been more than kind. Three years after my job, I got married, I really didn't think it would be easy for me to get married. However probably the girl who married me and her parents must have considered everything before they agreed.

Three years after marriage we were blessed with our one and only child, a beautiful daughter who gave us a lot of love. The job itself at Air India though difficult at times, gave me a lot. I finally retired from Air India in February 2017 and thanks to my parents, Air India and support from my wife and family, today I lack nothing. We have our own little flat, enough to eat, we have had a lot of holidays within India and abroad, thanks to the rebated tickets provided by Air India.

So, **I want my story to inspire those who today may think that they are down and out. I would like to assure them that the Lord who gave us life will definitely look after us.**

We should put in our effort for sure, that is the right thing to do. However, if we fail, once or twice, it doesn't mean we will not succeed. My mother used to always tell me "Failures are the pillars of success". When we are going through the darkest moments in life, it feels terrible, but we must not give up. Many a times doors will open when you least expect it. I would like to add another small paragraph. During the time I had done very badly in college and knew I was going to fail, I went into a shell, into a depression, I did not want to be with anyone, I did not want to talk to anybody. It was the time of vacation after the exams and my parents had planned a vacation to Darjeeling and Sikkim. I of course was very morose and by myself. We drove from Darjeeling to Gangtok and on the way, just a little detour was a famous Tibetan monastery in a place called Rumtek. The Lama of Rumtek was considered to be next only to the Dalai Lama. Seeing my condition my father took me with him to the monastery and we were fortunate to have an audience with the Lama. So, the Lama asked me, what is your worry? I told him I will fail and then won't get a job, and what will happen to me, I won't have any resources for making ends meet. When he heard me, his response was a hearty laugh. I was taken aback. Now I realise, The Lord that sends everyone to the world, gives them life, also looks after them. My religion Sikhism also tells us the same thing.

Thank you for taking the time to read this.

The Gambling Experience

We had travelled to USA for a vacation. My daughter Arshiya must have been 4 or 5 years old at the time and so the year would have been 1994, I think. My sister was working in the Washington D. C area. We had a home to go to where we would be welcome. I was employed with Air India and had access to rebated tickets, so we were excited to go. It was perhaps my daughter's first or second visit to USA, I'm not sure. Soon after reaching my sister, Manjula, chalked out our program on what all we should be doing. A cousin, also staying in Washington, was keen to go to Atlantic city and when she offered to take us, we decided to accompany her in the car. We had a great time. We that is, Preeti, my wife, and myself had been to Atlantic City earlier on a previous trip to America and we had enjoyed the experience. This time we took turns in playing at the casino as one of us would stay out to look after Arshiya, who being a child, was not allowed inside. Sometimes Manjula would look after Arshiya and both Preeti and me were together at the casino. Manjula was very clear in her mind, she felt it's better to spend some money on something more worthwhile such as food and soft drinks, ice cream and the like rather than waste it away in gambling. Time was passing nicely, playing at the casino, sometimes lucky, sometimes not. By the time it was time to go back we were up by about 70 Dollars, which to me was a lot of money! Atlantic city is like a mini-Las Vegas, it is by the beach and there are a lot of beautiful buildings. There are many casinos and hotels and it is a nice place for an outing even if you don't want to indulge in gambling. It is generally frequented by elderly Americans who like to pass their time and money having some fun. They have time and money to spare!

The casinos also encourage them by including a free coupon worth 20 dollars or so, in the return bus fare from nearby cities like Washington D. C. or New York. So, in effect it is almost a free bus ride! The coupon can be redeemed at the casinos for playing at the gambling tables. There are many gambling options available, slot machines, card games, roulette, to name a few. Reality of Words Publication So, after a satisfying full day's outing at Atlantic city, we reached back Manjula's house in Washington. The next day's program was already decided, we had been invited for lunch by another relative. I spoke to Preeti and Manjula and told them," You all go for lunch, I will go to Atlantic city again and earn some more money! I know how to make money". They were not too happy about it, but seeing I was very keen, they agreed. I convinced them as I was absolutely convinced that I know the formula for making money from gambling! I took the early morning bus and travelled to Atlantic City to make my fortune! I was carrying my packed sandwiches with me. We reached the casinos and we had to be back at the bus by a certain time in the evening. We were now on our own, i.e., me by myself, and the other bus passengers. I had carried with me all the money which I had brought with me for our holiday from India,700 Dollars in all. A vast sum of money in those days. My strategy was simple, I was going to bet on roulette and I would bet on either an odd or even number and would start with the minimum bet and would stick to the same option, even or odd. The roulette wheel has different numbers and colours on it. There is a small ball which is put on the rotating wheel and it ultimately comes to rest on a particular number. Now I had learnt probability in school and if there are only two choices, say odd or even, the probability of a number continuously coming again and again on odd, if a largish number of trials are conducted is very less. In fact, the probability each time is fifty percent, and in a large number of tries, it cannot each time continue to come on odd again and again and again. So, I thought I knew how to win.

I was simply going to keep on doubling my money on odd, if I lost the first time, and would keep betting on an odd number as it was sure to come one time at least. That way I would have got all my money back plus whatever amount initially bet. There were a number of names of the casinos. Ballys, Caesars, Taj Mahal, Trumps Casinos were some of the popular ones which I remember. I don't know which one I entered. I went straight to the Roulette table and got my coupons. Since it was not crowded as it was morning there was only me on that table. I had no option but to play alone. So, I was told that the minimum bet was 10 dollars, I think. I placed My ten-dollar chip on odd, the wheel was spun, I lost. I now put 20 dollars, lost again, now I put 40 dollars, again lost. It was unbelievable, but in a short span of five minutes or so, I had gambled away all my money!! I didn't win even once, had I won, I would have got all my money back. I am sure they had manipulated where the ball would stop! But there was nothing I could do. I was devastated!! You could well imagine my situation!! In the space of five minutes, I had frittered away all our money!! But what could I do. It was my own fault. I could blame nobody else; I had insisted to come here. I had simply been totally foolish!! So now I had to pass away many hours at Atlantic city, with no money and nothing to do! I just sat somewhere and moped on what I had just done. I didn't cry, but I really felt very bad and sad. I felt not only have I spoilt my holiday, but also the holiday of my wife and daughter for no fault of theirs. I had learnt a very bitter lesson. I think I must have felt similar to what Yudhishtir, from the Mahabharat would have felt when he lost everything including his wife

Draupadi in a gambling game with his cousins. The hours spent at Atlantic city seemed endless and the bus journey back to Washington was equally painful. I reached the Bus terminal and I had no money to take a cab home. I had no money to even make a phone call. I then made a collect call to my sister. A collect call is one where you can make a call and the phone company asks the receiver if they will accept the call and also pay for it. I told Manjula my sob story. Anyway, she guided me and I took a cab and reached her home and she paid the cab driver. It was a bitter, bitter experience, the only good which came out was!! No more gambling for me. For life!! Hope you all enjoyed reading my story. Hope you learnt a lesson from it!! You can never win at a casino!! If perchance you do win a little, just walk away. Better still, don't gamble at all!! There are better ways to use your hard-earned money!!

Gymkhana Memories

Such fond memories of the club!! Let me start by how I become a member. Of course, I became a member because my father, late S. Pritam Singh jee became a member years and years ago. There is an interesting story to how he became a member. He wasn't much the social type, however my mother was. My father was in the Government Service, one of India's distinguished Engineers, who retired as Chairman of Central Water Commission. My mother knew that Govt Service and Armed Forces officers get membership to the club on priority, she had been asking my father to apply. This was in the Seventies. My father had been resisting, he actually felt that Gymkhana Club members might be the snobbish types! Anyway, he finally applied and sure enough, my parents, were called at the "At Home". One of the committee members asked my father, "You have been in the Government for so long, and were in Delhi most of the time, why didn't you apply earlier?" My father, ever truthful started saying, "I was never interested! "And promptly my mother gave him a mild kick from under the table! She thought, such an answer would surely jeopardize the chances for membership!! Fortunately, they cleared this hurdle. And so he became a member. Of course, then we, as children could also use the club as dependents. So, I started using the club, the beautiful library, the squash courts, tried my hand at tennis and Swimming too! I have fond memories of the billiards room! And the bridge room! And the pool! I will start with the billiards. I had never played this game, and so the first few times I played on the "third table" with one of the markers, there was Morgan, Elias or Ilyas (everyone pronounced his name as such!) and a youngster then, Ramesh. Within a few days I saw another person and we started playing, my new found friend had just shifted base from London, Pakistan and now Delhi. He was a few years elder than me and had this fancy cue stick which he had got from London, the one which folds into two pieces and has a fancy case! I used to play with one of the club sticks. Our games were quite even and we struck up a friendship! He was the rich types and we were staying at South extension those days. My friend Sunil, was in Defence Colony. I had a two-wheeler Bajaj Scooter on which I would zip around; this was the time when the Maruti had recently introduced the Maruti 800 and the Maruti Van. My friend had an imported gaadi..and it had an amazing turning ability, let me not digress too much else this will get long and boring! So Sunil would call me and I would meet him outside Alliance Francoise and we would travel in style to the club! We would play billiards, snooker and side by side enjoy beer and finger chips! We would tell the waiter. Mote Alu. Liana!.Ah!.Those were fun filled enjoyable days!! My parents didn't mind too much as I would be out of their hair for a while! We got better and one day at the club tournament, it was sheer luck!! I got the highest break in Snooker and got a prize at the Sports Dinner! A very proud achievement for me.

I sometimes point out proudly to friends, take them to the billiards room...see my name is on the board!! Now of course I haven't played for ages and would be awful at the cue games! Coming to bridge! I started frequenting the bridge room, my mother was fond of it and I had learnt a little as a young boy as we used to play within the family while my father was posted to Kathmandu. So I used to be the youngest person playing in the bridge room amidst serious elders! I remember an incident vividly, I had dealt out the cards and I just pushed the cards nearer the other players as a good and polite gesture! However one of the players, a sophisticated white haired lady. Rani Sahiba of some place. I will not mention!! ..to keep the identity secret! ..well she gave me such a firing! "Don't you dare touch my cards!! she said. And she gave me such a cold look!! I could have frozen!!

Anyway, I enjoyed the bridge bouts and the sandwiches and the tea there!! Swimming! ..I didn't know how to swim, still don't actually, but had this great ambition to learn. We, Preeti, my wife and me made sure our daughter learnt, and we are very proud that Arshiya swims well. She was coached by Ashok and I asked Ashok." Will you teach me?" I was mortally scared of the water, still am..as I had once drowned at the AIIMS while in college and it was an experience I will never forget! My body had become all blue, I had blacked out and was in the water for a few minutes before I was fished out! This being the background, you can understand my desire to learn as well as anxiety! So, my understanding with Ashok was, I will be very happy and proud if I can do a length!! You all know the size of the pool. The lady Willington swimming bate!. Well with great pride and a lot of fear, I accomplished this heroic feat!! I was able to go from the shallow end till the deep end. But couldn't manage the way back!! So I accomplished my goal. And that was it for swimming!! Let me share my At Home Experience!! I had got married in 1986 and I think it was within a year or two of that we were asked to come for the At Home. As i was about to enter, a senior member, spotted me and said, are you going for the At Home. I said yet. He said where's your coat and tie!! I hadn't thought of wearing those or perhaps felt it wouldn't matter..!! He said, go change and come! I went all the way back home to Vasant Vihar, and came back, dressed adequately for the occasion! Of course we sailed through. Everybody does!! There are so many memories of this excellent club!! The Sunday buffet lunches!! We would gorge on the delicious food!! The family dinners together, Gymkhana was a favourite for our parents to entertain their guests! And we have followed this trait! I used to work for Air India, and at that time my office was at Ashok Hotel, a stones throw from the club. My routine was, play squash in the morning, take a shower and go to work! Lovely days!! The morning squash group by and large still is the same, sans me..I loved playing with JP, Deol Saab, Doc Rajeev, Ina, Chow, doubles was especially fun! And in Squash Tournaments too I got lucky!! In Lucky doubles, on two occasions, thanks to my partners! My name came up on the board!!

Then I discovered badminton, I didn't even know it existed in the club, well I started playing and took part in the tournaments, won a few prizes too, over the years! Not that I was good, but just that there was not too much competition! Especially in the Veterans! All in all, I have really enjoyed the club!! We get too meet friends at the bar! Enjoy the excellent programs put up by the entertainment committee from time to time! And last but not least. The bread!! We make it a point to get bread whenever we are at the club!! Waiting for the club to open fully!! Waiting for the Covid clouds to clear!! Looking forward to clubbing again!!

Hope you enjoyed reading!!

Accident 2.0

This time I hit someone! It was 13 January 2016. Our daughter Arshiya had got married to Naunidh Singh Arora just four days previously. It was supposed to be an auspicious day, the festival of "Lohri", is celebrated on that day. It is supposed to be the coldest winter night of the season and thereafter warmer days are expected to come. In the evening after sunset, family and friends gather together and light a bonfire and partake of peanuts and "gajak" and "revari", Indian sweet candies, made out of sesame seeds and "gurh" or sugar syrup. Singing and dancing around the fire are part of the festivities. Lohri is also celebrated as the crops are harvested. It is a festival of joy! For a newly married couple, the first Lohri festival post marriage is considered to be a special event. It was perhaps early afternoon, we had not had our lunch and both Preeti, my wife, and me were tired after the hectic wedding ceremonies and celebrations of the past few days. Preeti suggested that since it is the First Lohri of the married couple, we should get some gift hamper packed for the Arora's as we would be going to the Arora residence in the evening. I was tired but still this had to be done, either now or later. We decided to go to the RK Puram market to buy some fruit, some peanuts and revari, etc for the hamper, so that we could then rest and be fresh for the evening celebrations. On our way back home, I was at the wheel, driving my sister Manjula's car. Her car was running on CNG (compressed natural gas) considered to be less polluting than petrol or diesel. We had borrowed her car for the wedding as the Delhi Government, alarmed by the rising pollution levels had declared an odd even scheme for the cars. This meant that on an odd date, only cars with odd registration numbers could ply and on an even date, the cars with an even number were allowed.

There was an exception however for CNG cars which were allowed daily. Both our cars were with even number so we had requested Manjula to lend her car temporarily so that we could manage all the wedding functions easily. Reality of Words Publication It was an old model Honda City car. We were almost home and were in Vasant Kunj, B10 market area, crossing the market at a very slow speed due to heavy traffic around the place. I might have been at around 15 kmph not more. Suddenly there was a big noise and the car's front windscreen shattered! I stopped the car immediately to see what had happened and to my horror I saw a sickening sight. A man was bleeding heavily from the head, I had hit him, I don't know how as I had not seen anyone, perhaps he had tripped and fallen in the path of the car, perhaps I had dozed off while driving, I can't say. I was stunned and shocked. The person was bleeding profusely. My first thought was to take him as fast as possible to the hospital. A crowd gathered in seconds, without a thought, I took the help of some people and put the moaning, bleeding man on the back seat and told the crowd, I am taking him to Fortis Hospital.

The hospital was barely five minutes away and we rushed to Emergency. There was a car just behind me when the accident happened and the gentleman driving was very sympathetic to me, saying I was right behind you, and it's not your fault. I saw everything. If you like you can take my name and number for any help. In fact I think that gentleman followed me right up to Fortis hospital, Vasant Kunj. At the hospital, the doctors started attending to the man. They said we can't say anything about his state or his injuries right now, we will have to do a CT Scan. They had contacted the police too after finding out that it was an accident case.

There were a myriad of thoughts running inside my head since the accident happened. I feared the worst and was reconciled to whatever would happen. I was just praying for the life of the person. Praying that he should live. I had mentally accepted that I could be arrested and even put behind bars as they could make out a case of rash driving against me. Well, the police inspector arrived, a gentleman called Hukam Chand. He took my statement and wanted to question the victim but he was in no state to be able to talk.

In the meantime, Preeti did a wise thing and called Naunidh to tell him what had transpired. Naunidh, his elder brother and Mr Maninder Arora, Naunidh's father arrived at Fortis. This was a big moral support for me as Naunidh was a lawyer himself. They advised me not to volunteer any extra information to the police and not to accept that it was my fault. By now the patient was able to tell his employers telephone number. I called him up to tell him what had happened and where we were. It turned out that the victim was employed as a helper to a senior lawyer of the Delhi High Court. The lawyer took down my details. As suggested by Mr Arora I offered and paid an amount of Rs 20,000/- to the lawyer to cover for the immediate medical expenses. This was a big mental trauma for all of us, especially for me.

The inspector said he would have to impound the car and he took my license. We drove the car to the police station and parked it there. He took particulars of my sisters' details too as she was the car owner. Later my sister was called and she had to sign a paper too. We were told that now the person who was injured could either settle the matter out of court, or if they so desired, they could sue us and the matter would be decided in court.

We spoke to the lawyer and discussed the matter of resolving the issue out of court, but he declined. All along I just kept praying for the life of the person who had been hit. It was already evening time by now and Preeti and me, finally reached home, changed and went for the Lohri celebration.

You can imagine my state, I was not in any mood to celebrate, but it was necessary for me to be at the function. All the people close to the Arora family had been invited and I had to relate the event of the accident to them.

The next day I went to the hospital to enquire about the health of the victim. I was relieved to learn that he was out of danger. Naunidh's close friend and associate was a criminal lawyer and he represented me in the court proceedings. I had to go to the court a couple of times to appear before the judge. My sister too had to come once.

Reality of Words Publication In the meantime, the victim had been discharged and had resumed his daily activities. I called his employer and was asked to make some further payments for his treatment and medication.

Finally, the employer of the victim, the lawyer agreed to settle the case by mutual consent provided I paid Rs Two Lakhs as compensation. We discussed the matter and agreed to pay. Thus, I breathed a huge sigh of relief. I had suffered this time a lot more mentally than the time I had been a victim myself. That time I had endured the physical pain. This time it was the mental anguish that I faced. Thanks to Almighty that the victim got OK and the matter was settled out of court. Subsequently I was able to retrieve the car, we had to get new seat covers as the seat covers were badly stained with blood. I had to get a new windshield too. Thereafter I returned the car to my sister.

This was a brief true account of the accident. The whole episode from start to finish took about three months I think, a period of great uncertainty and worry for me!

The lesson to be learnt is, be careful when you drive. Never drive if you are feeling sleepy! In case you hit someone, and the person gets injured, take care of the person and don't run away. God will protect you from harm!

Demons

We all have demons, I'm pretty sure of that! And of course, I have my share too. Let me begin from the beginning, always a good place to start! As the years have gone by, from infancy to now, the demons in my life, have only increased, I'm now, a ripe 64! So, there are a few! In the beginning, an early demon was fear! I may have been around 4 years old... or even lesser at the time, when my father tested us children. He asked us, this was night time, and my number in the hierarchy of kids was number three. My brother was five years older than me, and my elder sister two years older and the smallest was only around 2 years old at that time. So, my father said, who will volunteer to go into the bathroom and stay in. With the lights off and the door locked from outside. For a moment none of us responded, then I took up the challenge!

And felt quite proud! My heart was beating faster than usual, but I fought my fear. And overcame it! This is not to say, that I was full of courage. Fear came in many forms! The fear of getting the horrible burning ointment put on my wounds as a child, the fear of getting an injection, the fear of getting reprimanded at school for not doing homework etc.

Let me move on to other demons. I am a Sikh and our religion talks of five big demons, Kaam, Krodh, Lobh, Moh, and Ahankar. The English translation being Lust, Anger, Greed, attachment and pride or ego. In my case, the first one is a big issue. I find it difficult to overcome. In today's time of the free world and the internet, it is easy to get swayed. There are many temptations. I truly believe, you will get the fruit of your actions, both good and bad. And I remember vividly all the wrong things I have done. And they keep tormenting me.

Many of my sins, are not crimes. But they should not have been done. I knew it then, but still did those things, and I'm sure these demons and sins, will continue till the end. When I at times overcome the demons, that gives me a great feeling. And I will continue my efforts, to deal with them, to fight with them.

Actually, I prefer not to talk to my demons, it's best not to think of them. It's better to stay far from then. But every now and then, quite suddenly, a demon will come. And that is the biggest challenge. The only thing which can save me, and not add to my woes, is to take the support of the Almighty. Only He can help me! If I remember Him, He will give me strength, and banish these demons, from my life. KAAM

One of my big demons is lust. It is known as Kaam in Punjabi. I have to fight with this demon a lot, sometimes I win, at times I don't.

I normally confront this demon when I am alone, and especially at night. I am very attracted to the opposite sex however since I was quite shy, I did not make many friends with girls.

Even now, I am married but still this demon confronts me. In today's open world and as everything is easily available on the internet, it is easy to get tempted and watch what one is looking for. The issue is, I know this is not right, and if I do indulge, later I feel bad. Of course, one can justify anything, but this demon has been troubling me since many years

The Ideal

From my diary of 1991 2 or three wrote for myself. However, it is easy to preach but difficult to follow The Ideal A fit and healthy person Ever thankful and grateful to God. Always, aware and filled with His presence Naturally such a person will not do anything contrary to what his conscience dictates.

Try to do some exercise or play some game every day. Try and use the bicycle as often as possible. Eat within limits-avoid sugar, excess salt, fried things, eggs, milk and butter.

A God filled person needs nothing else in life. God has given me everything. One should try not to ask favours from anybody. Begging is out of the question. A person who is satisfied will be happy. Money is not very important as many poor people are happier than people having a lot of wealth.

Trust is very important in life. One must trust one's closest ones fully and completely. Try and get up early in the morning, say 5am on the days possible and meditate. As often as possible visit the gurdwara. As often as possible try and help the needy. Try and have a bath every day if possible early morning with cold water. Brush your teeth twice a day or more often.

There is nothing wrong in trying to improve your status or in trying to earn more. Try and be nice to people. Try not to lose your cool. One should not cow down under any threats. One should not be afraid of anything or anybody. One should not get excited about anything but should remain cool.

There are a lot of things to be learnt in life. A lot of knowledge to be imbibed. Try and be more aware of things around. One should try not to be inquisitive about people's private affairs. One should not try and interfere with anybody else's life.

One should try and respect everybody regardless of their status or colour. There is nothing good or bad, everything is relative. What one person feels is good another may feel is bad or what one person condemns another person may not.

One should live with oneself and God. Be your own best friend. You know yourself as nobody else does. You know your strengths and weaknesses. You know all the sins and dirty deeds that you have committed. Try with God's grace to do nothing against your conscience.

Do not give into temptations. One should never feel superior to anybody else. We all have a lot of goodness and also weaknesses. Do not expect anything in return for any favours you think you have given to anybody. Try and be as independent and self-sufficient as possible.

Try and be courteous and respectful to elders especially parents and in laws.

Try not to get provoked. Try not to talk about yourself, never boast about yourself. God has looked after me thus far very well and will continue to do so forever. He looks after not only me but everybody and everything. He has given everybody a conscience and if we do not listen to our conscience. We will be going against him and will definitely get repercussions. All our actions and thoughts are known to God.

Try and not talk ill of anybody especially behind their back. Try and live life as fully as possible. Time once lost is lost forever. There is no need to worry about anything at all, try not to be attached to anybody too much.

Some Thoughts

Am writing, whatever thoughts that are coming to mind. I'm 62 years old, don't know how many or who will read, what I have to say.

We are here for a brief instant in time, yet we feel, we will never die. We like to show off, to prove we know better.

Our entire life, we try to win arguments, to show we are more intelligent, or knowledgeable. We try and amass wealth, goods, status. And we feel, when we will have all these material things, a home, a car, a nice phone, good clothes, a swanky job, we will then be happy.

Perhaps we will, but it would be better, if we find happiness everywhere, every day, even in sorrow, or in difficult times.

I see so many, very wealthy people who have all the material possessions, enough to last, many lifetimes, yet they are not happy! Something is missing in their life, maybe their children haven't turned out nice, perhaps they have health issues, or they are not at peace with themselves.

What is it that can make one happy? Is it possible to be happy? All the time? What is one's goal in life, being happy I guess, is a worthy goal. Since I am older than most people who will read this, I can always offer some advice, it is a different matter, that I may not follow my own advice!

We all are born, out of love or passion, we need to be thankful to our parents, who brought us into this world? Life comes about this way, for all. There are so many different species in the world, we do not even have the capacity or knowledge to name them all, leave alone know about them.

Humans are supposed to be the most intelligent of all the species, perhaps they are. However, they have not been intelligent over the years; I can say this with conviction, having read some history.

I have read, there were many wars, millions were killed in the name of religion, or because of greed, or someone thought I am the greatest and want to conquer the world.

In the process, millions lost their father, brother or husband. Wars only brought misery to people, no one really wins in a war.

If man was truly intelligent, he wouldn't have thought of war. Should not man have realized, we are here only for a few years. Some even do not reach the age of 20. But most people live 60,70, or 80 odd years. There are very few who may go past 90 or even hundred. However still, this is a very short period in the whole scheme of things. This earth, is millions of years old and we are here, only for a short while.

If man was really intelligent, he wouldn't, or all the countries would not spend so many of their precious resources on making weapons or buying weapons.

Should not have all the leaders of the world realized, there are many more important matters to attend to. Consider this, the earth so far is the only place in the whole Universe which is capable of sustaining life. We are a small planet in the solar system and we know through science that there are millions of stars and galaxies, so in that sense, Earth, so small a placer, is unique and wonderful!

Yet we continue to destroy this beautiful planet. We have spoilt the environment. Due to our greed, we have cut down millions of trees. We have been polluting this beautiful place, by burning, wood, oil and producing poisonous fumes.

The Ozone layer, given by nature is depleting giving rise to huge environmental problems. The Air in the cities we are breathing is hazardous. We produce so much waste, we have actually built mountains of waste.

How can we call ourselves intelligent! If we were truly intelligent, all the leaders of the world would have sat together and discussed and decided that there would be no more wars. No more producing Nuclear weapons. Perhaps they all should have decided, there will be only one army in the world, made up of soldiers from all the countries, and if and when, there is any trouble, or unrest, anywhere in the world, this world army would go, and sort it out.

The International Court of Justice could decide and adjudicate of matters of strife, all over the world. Who knows, perhaps we will reach there one day. Some years ago, when Russia and America mutually decided to cut down on nuclear weapons, it was a step in the right direction.

A recent example of man's stupidity is the millions of people killed during the partition of India. Could not this have been done, in a much better way? Hopefully man will learn from all the mistakes he has made in the past.

On Happiness

A simple solution for happiness, I feel is, it should start with the individual. If all of us are happy, if we all do the right thing, there would be no trouble at all! How is this possible? Well for a start, we should not differentiate between people, by colour, race, religion or sex. All children should get education, it doesn't matter if they are poor or rich.

This way there will be equal opportunity for all children. People can choose their profession on the basis of their likes or aptitude. A nation needs all kinds of workers. And no job should be considered small. In other words, there should be dignity of labour.

The family should be the basis and the starting point from where happiness would originate. The most important member of the family is the mother. From mothers are we all born and we get nutrition from them.

For any country to develop, it is so important that all women are educated. Women are mothers and would-be mothers. Once they are educated, they become aware of so many things. Thus, they can raise their children in the right way.

It is well established that only a happy person can spread happiness and no one else. As they say, charity begins at home. So also, happiness begins at home. A happy mother will bring up a happy child, will inculcate the right values and this way, if all homes bring up happy children, society nations and the whole world, will be a happier place.

Of course, the world is not perfect and as evident from the past, there will always be a mix of the good and the bad. My own formula for being happy, goes something like this.

Our happiness depends on us alone. At least it should. We should not give the power to anyone else to affect our happiness. One of the main reasons of being unhappy is that we have expectations from people. If we stop expecting anything from people, we will never be disappointed. And whenever we will get something, we will feel good. And when we don't get, we will not be sad, because we never expected anyway. The words of Lord Krishna come to mind. Who while guiding Arjun said, do your duty. But leave the result to God. The result is not in your hands. But you must do your duty. As best as you can. So, in my case, I try not to expect; even from my wife or daughter, or from friends.

One other thing I have noticed is, when we make someone smile, or laugh, or make anyone happy, that makes me happy too! Economics teaches us that man has unlimited wants, and scarce resources. Economics is all about maximizing these wants from the scarce resources. In my view, if we twist this around a bit, that is, if we can limit our wants and if we feel our resources, (God given,) are unlimited, we will always be happy.

I will share a little story, once there was a man, very dejected and sad, and he felt like committing suicide, and as he was about to do so, he met another man, who asked him, why are you so sad. He said, I have nothing now, I have lost my job, I have no money, my wife and me don't get along, I have nothing, so I am going to end my life.

The other man said, you may do as you wish, but before that, can you give me something? The man said, what can I give you, I have nothing. The other man said, give me your eye. Then the man realized...yes there were so many things he had, which he took for granted, like his eyes, his capacity to think, his body, his limbs, his ears, his capacity to speak etc.

We need to be aware, we have so much to be grateful for! When we came into this world, we had nothing. And when we go, we will be taking nothing with us. All this property and money and possessions and family, nothing will go with you! Perhaps the only thing that will go with you, is your karma.

You will reap, whatever you sow, that is karma. Quite like every action has an equal and opposite reaction. This is why all religions teach us, do good things, eschew the bad, you will be called to judgement at the end, and on that will depend, whether you go to heaven or hell. We may not believe in the above, but this is definitely true, whatever bad things you do or whatever sins you commit, even if no one knows about them, will always haunt you and trouble you.

It is best to forgive, to forgive others. And also, to forgive yourself. For believers in God, this helps a lot, as God is all forgiving. Try and not repeat, the mistakes of the past, every day is new, and brings an opportunity to improve. I will wind up now, and try to summarize, what works for me, to be happy.

1. Don't expect.

2. Be grateful. God has given you everything. More than you need, and also more than many others, be grateful for your good home, your parents, your good health, for the food you eat every day, for the cup of tea! for the friends you have, etc.

3. **Do the right thing.** That is listen to your conscience.

4. **Enjoy all the moments**. Appreciate all the beauty around you, the beautiful Sunrise and sunset, the plants, the birds, the flowers, the leaves. There is a lot of beauty. So many wonderful trees. And all this is free.

5. **Spread joy and happiness, help people if you can, just a smile or sometimes just listening to them.**

6. **Learn from the past. But don't live in the past**

7. **Try to learn new things**. Realize how little you know; you could learn a new hobby, such as singing, painting, playing a new game, gardening etc.

8. **Appreciate people.** Try not to find fault with people.

9. **Respect**. Give respect to people, especially to those older than you, but also to everybody! Respect things as well, respect a pencil, pen or your badminton racquet by caring for them.

10. **Meditate.** That is take out time for yourself and be in peace. Remember and thank God. For everything! Thank God, for each new day. For all He has given you.

11. **Ego.** Curb your ego. Realize you are not so important. Do not throw your weight around. Nobody is big or small. It doesn't matter if a person is rich or poor. You are not greater than anyone else.

12. In my religion, they talk a lot of controlling the 5 bad things, Kaam, Krodh, Lobh, Moh and Ahankar. So be careful. Do not have lustful thoughts, curb your anger..it is just a d away from danger! Do not be greedy!

.. Do not be attached to anything too much. That will cause only pain. And lastly do not be proud. That is curb your ego!

A few more general things**, be patient**, think of all the tough times you have endured and be thankful for where you are now.

Learn from your failures, the biggest triumph is when you fall or fail, but get up again, and prove to yourself and others that you can do it! **Be in Chardi Kala**, it"s a phrase used in the Sikh community to denote, always be optimistic. Be happy.

Troubled times come in everyone's life but it is how we react to them that define us. Be aware that no time remains the same. After night, comes a new day. After darkness, light is just round the corner. Lead a balanced life, be aware that neither the joy or success will last for ever. Success and failure are just two sides of the coin.

The greatest scientists and inventors failed several times before they met success. I have just shared, what works for me. Like I said earlier, it is easy to preach!! But difficult to follow! And if perchance you fail, don't worry, just try, and try again!!

Thank you for taking the time to read this.

My Thoughts on Happiness

I'm happy now!
I remain happy...it wasn't always like this.

I'm 64 and a lot has happened in life, as it happens in everyone's life. I was very sad at one time, contemplated suicide too, felt ashamed of myself. Didn't want to look anyone in the eye. I wanted to avoid meeting people. I had done miserably in academics while in college and was very worried.

Cut to now, I've realized that I am happy. And I am happy every day, every moment rather. (Not quite true. Read on. You will find out)

How did this happen...
Perhaps my experiences will benefit someone... perhaps you can get something out of this book.

Don't we all want to be happy?
Yet how many of us are happy?
We see and we read and we hear stories every day, people are miserable and sad, even though they have plenty of money, a good job, a nice family and a good home.

Am sharing my experiences...

Read on!!

Why this book?

I write because I enjoy it! I'm happy just now while typing this!

In fact, I am happy most of the time, by that I mean I am content, I am at peace.

I don't know how many will pick up this book and read it. It doesn't really matter. I will be happy if people read it. I will be not be unhappy if people don't read it.

I write nothing new, nothing which you don't know about. But I do feel being content, being happy, being at peace are important, and I am writing from my own personal experience.

At the present moment too, there is a lot I could complain about! The weather…it is so hot!!

My pain in the knee, I was so happy in my routine of playing every day, one day, a couple of weeks ago, while playing squash, I had a bad injury, probably a muscle or hamstring tear. It was unbearable it happened all of a sudden without my bumping into anyone, I had just taken a step to pick up the shot hit by the opponent and suddenly I got this terrible pain.

I had to sit down and am now taking painkillers and undergoing physiotherapy, but I am not going to let this affect my being happy. Things could have been much worse. Perhaps this was Gods way of telling me, don't play squash. Stick to table tennis and badminton and cycling. Right now, I can't do any of these activities. That's ok. I am using the time to write this book!

What I'm trying to get at is simply this: one can accept any situation; one can be happy even when things are bad.

Let's talk about happiness. What is happiness? Can one remain happy all the time?

No, one cannot remain happy all the time. No one can be happy if he or she has lost someone close, a parent, a child, a friend or a pet. We cannot be happy if we are witness to an accident that has just happened. One cannot be happy if one has performed miserably at an exam and failed too. There can be so many examples, one cannot be happy if you feel guilty about something. One cannot be happy if someone close has betrayed you.

Then what am I talking about. When I talk of being happy at all the time, I actually mean being at peace. **Peace of Mind**. My father always used to say *Peace of Mind* is the most valuable gift that you can have.

Let me share my personal experience with you. I had a normal happy childhood. The third child of middle-class parents born in a Sikh family. We lived in Delhi, India. We were four siblings, boy..girl..boy.. girl in that order.

Everything was normal, until it came to the time of my school board exams. I was not a studious disciplined child and so I was in a state of deep funk just before the all-important exams. The year was 1976. Since I had not been studying regularly, I wasn't prepared and I tried to finish the course for the science subjects, economics and mathematics I had opted for by staying awake almost the whole night before each exam.

Obviously, I didn't do very well in the exams even though I managed a first division.

I joined a prestigious college called Shri Ram College of Commerce in Delhi University and took up Economics Honours. In those days unlike now it was fairly easy to get into college even if one didn't have 97 percent or above!

My daughter by the way is quite impressed that I got admission into SRCC!

Anyway, my problems with studying continued and ultimately, I failed in college not once but twice! You can understand how traumatic that would have been for me especially as all my siblings were doing well and my parents friends' children too were either becoming doctors or engineers, **I felt ashamed of myself**. Especially when they would ask my parents, what is Jagmit doing?

My father worked for the government so there was no way I could have joined my father's business or shop. Avenues for further studies or getting a job were blocked as in most courses like LLB or MBA a minimum percentage of 50 percent in graduation was required which I did not have.

During this time, I got very depressed and even contemplated suicide. I was worried, my parents were worried. I was unemployed and miserable as I ought to have graduated in 1979 but finally managed to graduate in 1981 and that too with a BA pass course degree instead of an honour's degree.

These were two long years during which I was unemployed and really doing nothing to earn a living whereas all friends and acquaintances were striding ahead in their respective fields.

For all my woes I started blaming my parents, "You changed so many schools, I was doing well in St Xavier's Kathmandu, Nepal but you changed my school! First you put me into Air Force Central School then one fine day into Modern School without my consent"

"I am staying in a room on the Barsati! (a room built on the terrace) It is so hot! There is no cooler or Air Conditioner. How can I study?" All excuses of course, not admitting that I just wasted my time and also took to some bad habits.

"You did not discipline me"

I was not man enough to admit that the fault was mine. I blamed the college lecturers that they did not come to teach, they were only whiling away their time in pursuit of IAS. The quality of teaching was bad etc.

Not admitting that instead of attending classes I used to spend more time in the college canteen!

During these turbulent years after I joined college till the time I got my first permanent job in July 1983, **two important events happened** in my life.

The Accident:

I had been given a scooter, Bajaj 150 on the condition that I would have to run errands for my parents when asked. One day while it was my time to play my mother told me to pick up my father from his office which was about 10 kilometres' away. I drove fast as it was evening time and I wanted to get back to play badminton. To my surprise my father was not in office so I felt very angry! My precious time had been wasted! I drove very fast, at 80 KMPH and on ring road just opposite a big government hospital called Safdarjung hospital I met with a terrible accident. I hit a fiat car **head on**, the car turned from the other side of the road to go into Kidwai Nagar colony, the driver a middle-aged south Indian gentleman probably did not see me so I banged into the side of the car at that speed. Just before I hit the car, I realised what was going to happen, but there was nothing I could do, it was a terrifying moment, and then my scooter front hit the car. I must have flown across the scooter and banged into the car face first. I was moaning and groaning and spitting out blood and teeth.

They took me to hospital and there were a few bones broken, my mouth had become so swollen just as big as a chimpanzee! Meanwhile a good Samaritan had gone to my parent's flat which was about 2 kilometres away as I had not become unconscious and had been able to give my parents address. I was inside the hospital for 10 long uncomfortable days and was fed through the nose by a tube called Ryle's tube.

The accident came in handy as an excuse! **I failed because of the accident! I missed classes!**

The Drowning:

The second incident was a case of near death too, this time by drowning. I did not know swimming and my friend offered to teach me at an Olympic sized pool at AIIMS. (All India Institute for Medical Sciences) where he was studying for his MBBS degree. After a couple of days at trying to learn in the shallow end of the pool, my friend suggested come to the deep end. "It is easier to learn there." Much against my wishes and against my better judgement, I went to the deep end by clinging against the wall and tried to do a breadth.

Since I did not know how to swim, I went down, then came up but my head was submerged, after a few seconds of this horrifying ordeal which was actually like staring at death! I was also wondering why my friend is not saving me...I passed out!

I must have been in the pool in that state for a few minutes maybe five minutes or so.

The next thing I know I was lying tummy down by the side of the pool and had a big smile on my face as I gained consciousness while someone was pressing my body. I remember while I was drowning, I had the good sense not to swallow any water. There were a few people around me and my friend said my body had become all blue. It was the coach who had saved my life. I had not seen the coach before and he was not around when this episode happened. I asked my friend why he didn't save me; the answer was." I would have drowned myself" He had in the meantime made a noise and I'm sure the other people around would have made efforts to look for the coach. Apparently, the coach used a wooden pole to fish me out!

Both the above events left a deep impact on me. The accident meant countless visits to the dentist! The drowning has left a deep fear of water! I still do not know how to swim, though I did try as I wanted to overcome the fear and the happiest day of my life was when I managed to do a length of the Delhi Gymkhana swimming pool which is actually a very small pool from the shallow end to the deep end. When I tried to swim back, I could not manage and the coach helped me to bring me to safety. The effort to complete that swim was too much for me! Both mentally and physically it had drained me! Though on completing that one length I experienced pure joy!

I got my first and last permanent job in July 1983.

While I was jobless, I tried to learn some French, played a lot of billiards and snooker, played badminton took some coaching classes to prepare for IAS (Indian Administrative Service) managed to clear the Preliminary exam but could not pass the main exam.

11th July 1983, was my first day at Air India. I retired from Air India on 28 Feb 2017. More than three decades of work!

While I was unemployed and after failing, the thoughts in my mind were," what will become of me?" I wanted to drive an autorickshaw or a taxi to earn a living as I knew how to drive.

I also thought no one will marry me, because I don't have a job. During this phase I went through bouts of severe depression and also euphoria, I had to be taken to a psychiatrist and though I thought there is nothing wrong with me, I refused to take any medicine, but I later realised my mother was putting some drops (Serenace) without my knowledge in my milk.

Another fact I want to highlight here is I was very shy and plump too while in school. I would not talk to girls though I liked them.

My mental condition then was like this:
I was so morose and sad.

Didn't want to show my face.
I thought the best solution is.
I should die!

How to be Happy?

I am now going to write how I am in this state now. *A Peace of Mind State.*

Today: I am sixty-four years old; **actually young! With a lot of experience!**

I don't get angry too fast; I don't get too happy or too sad. I believe in God a lot.

I pray every day. Though I am by and large content, I do falter at times as I know only too well that I am human and have so many faults!

My suggestions are based on my experiences on how to be in a state of Peace of Mind.

I am going to write my thoughts on this subject and write the things I feel are important in **bold.**

Here goes!

Accept everything that happens in your life. There is no point in worrying or lamenting about the past. Yes, we can learn lessons from our mistakes and make efforts to try and not repeat them, but that is all.

Someone has so rightly said. Accept the things you cannot change. Change the situation if you can, if you can't just accept it or rise above it.

Many things are out of our control, we cannot do anything about it. The war in Ukraine, for example, the war should not have happened, but you and I cannot do anything to prevent it. No need to be unhappy because of this situation. Accept it.

Think of what you have at this moment. You have your body working fine, you are mentally fine too. You are able to see, to eat and enjoy so many flavoursome foods. You are able to read. People take these things for granted. Just go to the hospital and see patients there struggling for so many things, some of them even in that condition are happy and smiling! Hats off to them!

The most liberating and best thing for all of us is this:

Every moment is fresh and new!

Be in the moment, every moment.

Once there was a man, very morose depressed and upset with life. He had lost his job, had issues with his wife, was in debt and could see no way out. He set out to commit suicide. On the way he met a man who asked him, "Where are you going?" He answered saying "I am going to commit suicide as I have lost everything in life"

The man said, sure do what you think is best. "You say you have lost everything, can you do me a favour?" The man answered "What favour can I do for you? I have nothing to offer"

The man said," you have two eyes, just give me one of them!"

This led the man to think, he thought I have eyes, hands, feet and I can think. The words of this man made him realise that he had a healthy body and age on his side. He could make efforts and rebuild his life.

The most liberating and profound discovery.

For myself that is...
Each moment is new.
Each moment is fresh.
Each moment has a new flavour.
Each moment is a new opportunity.
Moments will come and go.
They are purely momentary.
Make the moment count.
Your life is just a moment too.

Make it count.

From this moment.
Forget about the moment's past.
They did not last.
They are gone and lost forever.
Make this moment count!!

The moment of sadness..
Has gone..
The moment of madness..

Has gone..
The moment of sin..
Is over..
The moment of cheap pleasure..
Is over..
That moment of lust..
Is over..
The moment of anger..
Has disappeared..
The moment of jealousy..
That too has gone..
The moment of attachment..
Get rid of it..
The moment of pride..
Has vanished..

The moment to give..
Is here..
Give your love..
Give your time..
Give whatever gifts you can..
The moment of bliss and joy..
Is here!!

Each moment is new.
Each moment is fresh.
Make each moment momentous.
Fill Each moment with joy!

Each moment is different.
A moment lost Is lost forever.
A moment of anger...
Can lead to disaster.

Fill your life with perfect moments.
It is fun. Satisfying.

How can that happen.

It's easy if you try.

Just remember the One.
Who gave you all these precious moments.
Moments with your mother.
The love of your father.
The moments with friends.

I'm stuck in the moment.
Fond of every moment.
I just love the moments.

Forgive me.
If I ramble too long..
Just take a moment.
Read this please.
Won't take long..
Just a moment!

The point I'm trying to make is this. **Be in gratitude always!**

The very fact that you are reading this means that you are alive. That is reason enough to be grateful. Life is a great opportunity! Life is about getting and giving joy.

There is a difference between pleasure and joy. Pleasure is momentary whereas joy is permanent. There is pleasure in possessing expensive things, however all physical things are temporary, nothing lasts, things go bad, things get lost. Joy is something that springs from within you. Joy is when you are in gratitude.

Think of all your blessings! When you were born, you got your body and mind for free. You got your parents for free; they raised you and made you into an independent person. When you leave this world, like all of us will, you will carry with you nothing!

Make the most of the moments which have been given to you! A moment lost is lost forever, it will never come back. If you believe in God, please understand that God wants you to be happy! In my religion Sikhism, they end the prayer with" Nanak Naam Chardi Kala, Terey Bhaaney Sarbat Da Bhala!" Which means Dear God I pray that I may be in good spirits and I wish for the welfare of all.

Even if you don't believe in God, its ok, but you do know it makes good sense to be in joy while you have this life. So just be in the present moment. Think of all that you have. Realise that at the present moment you lack nothing!

Don't think of the past and don't worry about the future.

Your happiness lies in your own hands. This is absolutely true. This is very powerful too; this means we don't give anyone else the power to affect our happiness.

Someone may try to hurt you with their verbal taunts, but if we choose to just ignore them and not react or get influenced, we will not let our happiness be affected.

Don't ask why people are hurting you, ask why are you allowing!

Do not have expectations from people. This is a difficult thing to achieve but it is very rewarding. If we don't expect anything from anybody, we will never be disappointed. Further if someone gives us something by way of kind words or a gift which we had no expectations of, we will feel good.

Lesson from the Geeta

In the Geeta Lord Krishna is advising Arjun after Arjun has told the lord that he cannot take up arms against his own close relatives and Guru.

Krishna counsels him and says "You as a Kshatriya must do your duty and fight for what is right, do your duty but leave the result to God."

In life we must try and follow this principle.

Introspect and see which have been the saddest moments of your life.

If you journey into your own life, you will realise that your unhappiest moments were those when you did what you should not have done.

Perhaps you had wronged someone. Perhaps you had hurt someone. Perhaps you had cheated someone. Perhaps you had been the cause of someone's misery.

You cannot change what has happened but you can surely learn from your mistakes and thus avoid these things. This is an important path to your happiness and peace of mind.

Believe in yourself.

Be yourself. Do not put on an act. Do whatever you think is the right thing to do. This will give you great peace of mind. Rabindra Nath Tagore famously said in his song " Akla Chalo Re" Go ahead and do the right thing, even if all others do not agree with you.

I am writing all those things which work for me.

Everyone is different, but perhaps you could try out some of the things that have worked for me.

Trust People

No relationship can work without trust. If you are married and you don't trust your spouse, the marriage will never work. The same is true of friendship. In every matter you have to trust people, for example if your car gets spoilt and the mechanic tells you that a certain part needs replacement, you have to trust him. This is not to say that you should be foolish and not do a little bit of research, you should ask your trusted friends or relatives, "can you suggest a good mechanic" Things like that. I am pointing out simple things which you would already be aware of. These simple things are very useful and important.

Humility

This is so important and will help you attain peace of mind. My grandfather was one of the nicest people I knew. I told him " Bauji tussi bahut acchey ho" "You are very nice " He didn't like me saying that. He said " Main nahi accha, Rab Accha hai" meaning " I am not good, God is good!" That is how humble he was.

If you are simple, unassuming and humble, you will get a lot of affection. This will add to your happiness.

Ego ..the five vices

This is quite the opposite of being humble. In my religion there is mention of the 5 vices. "Kaam, Krodh, Lobh, Moh and Ahankar" Lust, Anger, Greed, Attachment and Pride.

If we can get rid of these, we would attain peace. They are very difficult to overcome but we should try. For me the first one is really difficult that is Lust. Ego or the feeling of being important leads to a lot of problems." How dare he speak to me like that!" "Who is he to tell me what to do!" These kinds of reactions hurt your ego. If we can remove our ego most of the problems in the world will get sorted.

Truthfulness

If we speak the truth, we will never have to think before we speak. Sometimes it may be difficult to speak the truth but it will always help in the long run. Sometimes to cover up your lie, you need to keep lying again and again and ultimately you will get caught out and lose someone's friendship or trust.

Keep your word

I attach a lot of importance to this. If you have said something or promised something, you should keep your word. This will give you great peace of mind. People will start believing in you.

Don't Judge People

Do not gossip or speak ill of people behind their backs. Don't judge people. The reason is simple, when we point a finger at anyone, there are three fingers and a thumb pointing right back at us! Who are we to judge anyone when we know we have so many faults of our own!

Love Yourself

You are your own best friend! If you do not enjoy your own company, you will not be happy. If you love yourself and enjoy your own company, you will never be unhappy. If you are a happy person, you will automatically spread your own happiness around.

Forgive

Forgive people who have wronged you. Forgive yourself too. If you cannot forgive yourself, you will not be able to move on. You will always feel guilty about your misdeeds of the past.

Similarly, if you forgive others, you will not feel the hurt.

Accept that you don't know many things

Don't try to show your knowledge and try to prove you are right. There is so much you don't know. In fact, if you think of it, you hardly know anything!

In my case I hardly know anything. This leaves so much scope for me to learn! I want to know something about my own language ie Gurmukhi. I wasn't taught that subject in school, though my parents and grandfather tried to teach me. Now I am taking lessons and am trying to learn. I try to read one page a day of Guru Granth Sahib jee too, to understand more about my own religion.

I don't know how many parts my car or my bicycle has, yet I enjoy using them. I don't know the various parts of the body, where they are located and how do they function. I can't even sometimes bang a nail into the wall properly, how little I know. Yet a lot of us act as if we know everything. We go to great lengths to prove we are right. We have a big ego.

Health

This is so important. If you are not in good health, nothing feels good. Look after your body and your health as best as possible. Eat the right food. Get enough sleep. Exercise well. Keep your brain active too.

Jealousy

Avoid comparing yourself to other people. If you feel jealous, you are only hurting yourself. Instead, if you can feel happy about other people's success, that will add to your joy.

Hobby:

Take up any activity which brings you joy, reading, writing, gardening, playing, anything!

You time will pass nicely. REMEMBER, an idle mind is a devil's workshop.

Don't bother about What will people think:

You can't do anything about what people think or say or do. Don't bother about them. They don't really care about you. It is important however to pay heed to what your family and those who truly care about you feel. Do what makes you feel happy!

See the Beauty:

If perchance you are feeling sad, or even if you are not. Just see the beauty all around you. The trees, the birds, the squirrels. They are so pretty, each leaf is so wonderful, it is a thing of beauty. Look at the beauty of the birds, their colour, their lovely chirping sound.

Look at the beauty inside yourself. Marvel at your senses. The fact you can see, hear and feel. Marvel at the fact that you can enjoy music, that each one of us has so much in common but we all are different, we look different. Marvel at the Maker! How could He make millions and millions of people each looking different from each other? Also, miraculously He makes some people look so alike, an outsider can't make out the difference.

I was thinking about all these things especially during the lockdown and more so when I had covid and was isolated. The day I walked out of the house after more than three weeks of isolation was a feeling of pure joy! I truly appreciated freedom the way a prisoner must be feeling after being free. The walk in the nearby park was so exhilarating!

Look at what you've got, it is enough, more than enough

If you look carefully, If you look at your body and if you look at your room and your family, you will realise you have everything.

First of all, if you are reading this, it means you have good eyesight, you know English, you have a love for reading. If you look at your body, you will see that you have all the organs in good condition, which means a lot. Your teeth don't hurt, your ears don't ache, you don't have a headache, your limbs are working fine, you might be having medicines, but that is a blessing too! It is to make sure you live a good and full life.

If you look at your family, you may be having a spouse, children, parents, and siblings. Not everyone is so fortunate.

If you look at your home and your room, you will realise you have so many things! A lot of things you haven't used in a while, many books you haven't read. Many clothes you have hardly worn. A lot of things which you don't know fully about. For example, so many features on your laptop or mobile phone you don't know about.

What I am getting at is simply this. There is no reason to feel bored! There is enough to do, enough to learn without taking a step outside or spending any money.

Make use of your resources! THIS WILL LEAD TO HAPPINESS!

Respect people. Respect things

Give respect and you will get respect! It is as simple as that.

Everyone, regardless of their stature deserve respect. Talk politely and nicely to everyone.

You will see that in turn everyone will be polite to you as well.

Even with physical non-living things, something as small as a pen or a pencil or even a rubber band. keep them properly, in the correct place, in other words, don't be careless and casual with them. Treat them with respect! When you need to use these things, you will always find them and they will function properly. This will add to your well-being.

Don't throw your weight around

Treat people the way you would want to be treated yourself. If you are a manager and addressing the person who cleans the office, do not shout at him or her. There is a way of talking. **It is not what you say. But how you say it which is important.**

You will earn the respect of everyone around you.

Make friends. Play games

I have benefited so much, as I have played differe nt games in my life and hopefully will continue playing them for long.

Whichever game I have played, apart from the enjoyment of playing that game, I have made friends. Enjoyment and friends, both are an important component of happiness.

In my childhood played marbles, flew kites! So much fun. Some of those people are still friends. Played table tennis, cricket badminton, squash, billiards, bridge, tennis and squash. Now recently played a game called Pickle ball! Friends made! Joy and happiness gained!

Have a hobby

This is so nice and important. My friend who is into painting and gardening is so happily spending her time! She loves to post pictures of her plants and paintings and it gives her so much joy!

Reading or writing, anything really, another friend does a lot of knitting and also loves to go on vacations to explore new places.

ANY HOBBY LEADS TO SATISFACTION AND ENJOYMENT.

In my case, I used to love collecting stamps, later started collecting records LP's, I still have this collection of over 200 records which I'm very proud of even if I don't listen to them, they are kept nicely in a wooden rack specially made for this purpose.

These days I have started learning my own language, Gurmukhi. It leads to so much joy and satisfaction.

Enjoy your own company

I read somewhere, on Budh Purnima, that Gautam Budh said, conquer yourself before you go out to conquer anyone else. Enjoy your own company. You are your own best friend. You will never feel lonely! Introspect a lot. Realise your weaknesses, accept them and try and overcome them. "Manjeete jag jeet! " which means if you are able to conquer your mind, you will conquer the world!

This is only possible if you introspect, I was lucky in a way that due to my job requirements I had to stay away from my family for three stints during my career with Air India. While it was not easy, it gave me sufficient time to reflect! Some people have said, if you know yourself, you will know God! That is how important it is! To spend time with yourself.

Meditate

Get up early morning before dawn. It is easy for me to do this at this age. I have to get up to pee! Jokes aside, spending early morning time in meditation or prayer, is a wonderful way to make your day.

Appreciate When we appreciate someone, that person feels good! Especially if it is from the heart. You cannot really fake appreciation, though many try! When someone feels good by something you say, it makes you feel good too!

Pay Attention. Eye contact When talking and listening to someone, pay them your full attention. This means you give them respect. Eye contact really helps. When a person gets complete attention, he or she feels nice and good, that nice and good feeling resonates back to you!

Avoid the phone while talking Don't play with your mobile when talking to someone. The point has just been elaborated above but needs reiteration as this a very common habit.

Enjoy your bath..enjoy while brushing your teeth Basically enjoy every moment!

Be mindful Try and be mindful in whatever it is you are doing. If you are chewing food, you can be mindful of the origin of the food, the hands which might have planted the seed, nurtured the crop, harvested, the transportation of the food, the chain till it ultimately reached your home and then was cooked. If we are mindful of things, we appreciate them even more.

I am writing some more suggestions that come to my mind that can lead to happiness. Many of these are obvious and self-explanatory and don't need elaboration.

Enjoy reading

Don't try to prove you are right

Avoid the company of Bullies, loud mouthed people and braggarts

Spend time with your close ones

Love the other species including birds and trees especially dogs

Learn a language

The maximum joy comes in giving

Seva

Purity of Heart

Help People

Take blessings of elders

Speak the truth Always

Sing..dance..cycle

Empty the clutter

Keep your word..say what you mean..mean what you say

Exercise walk

Do the right thing

Guilt

Health is wealth

Don't talk ill of people..avoid gossip

Forgive yourself..forgive others

Nobody is perfect

Try to avoid things which bring you misery.. even if you do..there is always hope..each moment is new

You will become good at what you practise

Slow down..see the immense beauty all around

The ultimate..abscence of desire

Waste not..want not

Never talk about your achievements

Pavan Guru paani pita..maata dharat mahat Respect Nature. Pavan means Air, so Air is the Guru, Paan means water, water is the father, Dharati is Mother Earth, treat earth as your mother.

The present moment is all you ever have

You are your own best friend

A deep faith..you are already connected

Give space

Do the things you think are right..right n wrong are subjective

Admit your fault and apologize

Introspect..see your shortcomings and make efforts to improve

Try not to hurt people or their feelings

Get up early in the morning..before dawn

If you love your own company..you will never be sad..any day or moment

Spend time with those who matter ..but give them space

Have patience

Learn to let go

The ability to be able to laugh at yourself..at your mistakes

Difference between pleasure and joy

There are many channels. Choose wisely

Do something for society

The lesser things you have. The more happy you will be

The more things you learn. The happier you will be

Read inspiring biographies

Don't be too concerned or happy about your bank balance

Your property..your cars or your watches

A sense of humour

Compassion

Create beauty and harmony

Talk nicely to people

Time is a big healer.

You reap what you sow

You can interpret any situation positively

Everything happens for the best

Everything is temporary. Pain too

Let things pass

You can always choose peace Anand. Pleasure and pain are not the only two options

Thank you for reading!

Some of the stuff you have read might be repetitive, please bear with me.

SOME THOUGHTS- CALL IT POETRY

The Ladies

The world would not exist at all..
If it weren't for the female species.
It wouldn't grow too.. Nor would it be
Any fun.

She is God's most beautiful creation..
So pretty and nice..
My mother.. My daughter.. My sisters
And wife.

And all my lady friends..
So much joy I get..
When they smile..
Or talk to me.

They are so sweet..
Have such a nice nature..
So efficient and such great creators
Of the most tasty dishes..
And their sweet voice..
Like honey.. Pouring down from the sky..
Like rain

I just want to say thanks..
To all the women in my life..
And all my lady friends.

Sorry

I am sorry
To have hurt you
At times I open my mouth
Without thinking, on the spur of the moment
And then it's too late
To recall what has been said

We have shared more than thirty years
We have each other only
And God knows how many more
We will share together
One of us will go first
Most likely it will be me

I am sorry again
For all the mistakes of the past
I will try
To change my self
So that I don't hurt you
Again

Please do not hold if in your heart
Let the past be past
Let each new day
Be a new beginning
Of life more pleasant and joyful

Thank you for tolerating me
I'm glad you are with me
Till my journey lasts

Daughter

One day.. Back in 89..
We were blessed..
With the sweetest gift..
A gift from God..
And appropriately..
As my father..
Read a page..
From shri Guru Granth Sahib jee..
The letter A was chosen.

We picked the name Arshiya..
Meaning heavenly..
For she was a treasure..
From the heavens.. Was she sent

She gave us immense joy..
Even as a young child..
She was angelic and sweet..
She gave us so much love..
Difficult it is to describe.

And then.. She went to school..
Learnt many things..
And did us proud..
By getting so many achievements.

Her mother made so many efforts..
To give her the best..
She learnt a lot..
Besides the lessons from school..
She learnt singing..

Was in the school choir..
She made many friends..
And loved dancing.

Fond of sports she was..
Badminton.. Table tennis..
And tennis.. She played..
Swimming she learnt..
Which made both of us so proud

She did well in school and college..
And got a good job..
I must mention here..
Her love for pets..
She loved Snoopy..
Played a lot with him..
And what was nice to see..
Her heart.. So soft and pure..
She loved to help..
Any dog in distress

She got married one day..
And as she had wanted..
She chose her husband..
Who lives in Delhi

We are proud of her..
For she is an ideal daughter..
Always thinking of us..
Giving us gifts

We can never forget..
The love she used to shower..
By making sweet cards..
And throwing surprises..
On our birthdays and Anniversaries

She is courageous..
She is brave..
She is a friend to her friends..
She tries to keep everyone..
Happy.. She does the right thing

May God shower on her..
All his blessings..
May she get good health and happiness..
When tough times will come..
As they do..
In every one's life..
May God give her the strength..
To pull through

May God shower on her..
All His blessings.
May she get good health and happiness..
We pray for her..
Every day.. And we will..
Love her..
Till we are there

Heroes

There are so many heroes..
That one could emulate..
Who live cheerfully..
Despite not having.. what all we got.

Not a well to do family..
Hardly any education..
And yet.. They are happy..
Working hard.. With no time to think..

Childhood Memories

Sleeping on the terrace,
Going for after dinner walks with parents,
Visiting other families.

Playing with friends,
Marbles, cricket,
Flying kites!
Playing other games like,
Pithu, Stapu, Hide and seek,
And Dark Room.

Reading comics and books,
Archie's, Mandrake, Phantom,
Enid Blyton, Billy Bunter, Tin Tin,
And the likes!
Graduating to Agatha Christie, Perry Mason,
Hardy Boys, Westerns!
James Hadley Chase,

Riding the bicycle,
Throwing water balloons at Holi,
Bursting crackers at Diwali!
Eating Orange Bars and drinking Fanta
And coke!

The thrill of eating out!
Going shopping at Batas for new shoes!
Playing Ludo, Snakes and Ladders,
Card games like Teen do Paanch!
There were no A/Cs or TVs,
Few cars! All we had to do was,

Go to school and play,
No need to study much!

I am recounting the Happy days,
When we were children,
Back in the Sixties and Seventies!

We enjoyed a lot!
The times were good,
There were no mobiles,
So people had time!
And drinking tap water,
Was considered just fine!

Thanks to our parents,
We had a great life,
And some friends of then,
Are still friends now!

That time was good,
This time is different,
But its still good,
It could be far worse,
Thank God for no wars!
Let this Corona thing go away,
For all times do not last!

Parents

My parents were worried,
I wasn't faring well in studies,
I was giving them sleepless nights,
It wasn't fair or right.

But that is what happened,
I wasn't myself I know,
I did things I shouldn't have,
But what could they do,
A grown up boy,
Couldn't even be slapped.

But all times pass,
Those times also didn't last,
God was kind, He gave me everything,
And with time,
Though I still played truant,
Perhaps I improved.

They were a class apart,
They took everything in their stride,
They never chastised me,
And I can never forget that.

They are not here now,
But I remember them a lot,
And I feel they are beside me,
And I know,
They will only see,
The good in me,

And will always overlook the bad.
Whether or not I deserve it,
I know,they will always be,
Proud of me.

Wife

We may fight..
But that's all right..
We may argue..
But I know..
You care..
And you know.. So do I..

We have given (each other). . Or rather got..
A wonderful and precious gift..
Our daughter..
And I have to thank you for that..
Thank you for being with me..
Tolerating me..
Helping me..

Life would be no fun alone..
You know..
I don't like to go out anywhere..
Without you..
Except.. Perhaps.. To play

I know I can depend on you..
To do the taxes.. And many things more..
You make good food..
Are efficient at managing the house..

And what I like a lot..
What you don't talk about..
You have achieved so much in life..
In you career and the like..
But you do not gloat over it..

You are much more intelligent than me..
But intelligent enough..
Not to show it

We have enjoyed a lot..
All our holidays..
Which would have been no fun..
Without you

So here's to you..
My feelings for you..
My darling wife..
Thank you..
For caring for me..
When I was.. Down and out.

You have your faults..
As we all have..
You are not all good..
And no body is..
But as compared to me..
You are, a Saint..
And very tall.

Glad to be with you..
Let's spend the remaining time..
Together.. With more love..
Thank you Preeti..
For everything!

Pour Your Heart

Fill your heart with love..
Pour it out..
You will find..
It doesn't diminish..
Just keeps getting filled!
It is just like the sun shining
Day after day after day
Sending its heat and light..
But not diminishing in its might!
There is one thing though
We must empty our heart
Of hatred and all negative thoughts
To make place..for all the good stuff!!
I have seen from close quarters
My mother..living like this
And I know it works..
Friendly and helpful
No hatred for anybody at all
Yes it's OK to hate..
Like my father did..
Sloth and injustice
Deceit and things like that

An Ode to Women

Are you an angel
Or are you a queen
You are the woman
Of my dreams

All the women, out there in the world,
Each one of you, so beautiful,
In your own special way.
Without you, there would be no joy,
Or life indeed.

From inside you, you give us,
Sweet babies, girls and boys.
You nurture them,
With all your love,
Disregarding your own care.

Women, you are beautiful!
So soft and pretty,
Such beautiful voices,
And amazing feelings too.

Please don't hurt their feelings,
Sometimes it happens,
Without meaning to.
She will forgive you later,
And make the world better,
For you and for me.

What more qualities should I write,
She cooks and bakes,

Makes achars and chutneys too.
Keeps the house clean,
But sometimes shouts at you!

When you are in the middle of something
Or just relaxing,
She will ask you to do something,
Can be quite irritating too.

But overall I can say,
Life wouldn't be pretty at all,
If it weren't for you!!

Carefree Child

Wish I could go back in time..
To be that carefree child..
Playing marbles and flying kites
With not a worry in sight
A joy to go out and play
How time flew then!
Unworried about the dirty nails
Coming back home..
Drinking water from the tap..or fridge
Not worried about crossing
Any bridge..
Unburdened ..with not many sins..
How I wish..
To be back in time..
To be that carefree child!

My Life in a Nut Shell

When I was a small child,
I was chubby,innocent and sweet,
As I grew bigger,
From a child to a young boy,
I learnt a little bit of deceit.
The teenage years came pretty soon,
Comparatively I was still more innocent than most,
To explain this further,
I will quote an example,
A friend asked me,
Do you know how,
Babies are born?
I wasn't quite sure,
I knew it had something to do,
With the tummy and the navel,
But to tell the truth,
I wasn't quite sure!
As I grew bigger,
Unforceable changes happened in the body,
Like voice change and others best not mentioned!
And I did realise,
A little more about sex,
And about how,
A new life comes about.
But I was shy,
And though I used to find girls very pretty,
But I didn't quite have the guts,
To talk to them,
Or tell them what was in my mind.

Then with college came a new found independence,
With more freedom and less restrictions,
Learnt some new tricks,
Best not mentioned!
Studies took a back seat,
Playing games and movies and just hanging out,
Got more prominent.
With poor marks,
Opportunity got restricted,
While peers moved on,
My life came to a standstill.
The tough and depressing years passed,
And then I found a job!
And i held on to that for three decades,
Until I found myself retired.
Of course with the job,
A little after,
I found a marriage partner,
And the best time came,
When we had the sweetest child!
And now in these golden years,
Should i say twilight of my life,
I reflect back and think,
I was lucky! It must have been fate,
Or the hand of God!
That I think,I have led a varied life,
Many regrets,some joys too,
Most of all a lot of gratitude!
There is some time left,
Not quite sure how much,
But its my effort now,
To try and make the most,
Of the remaining time to be spent,
On mother Earth!

Me and You

I am in my own space,
As you are in yours,
Don't try to change me,
If anything, change yourself.
Do not judge me,
As I do not judge you,
If anything, judge yourself

Birthday

Born 62 years ago..
A product of my parents love..
Nurtured so well..
From an infant..to a boy..
Adoloscence..difficult..teenage years..
To a grown up man..
All through they loved me..
So so much...
They are not here now..
I'm everything..because of them..
I know I fell short..that was my fault..
I remember them..they always
Held my hand..wonderful parents
God gave to me..He called them back
That is Life!!
Their love..which got into me..
I'd like to spread it wide..
From the heavens they will see..
And smile..and say..
That is my child!!
A grown up man now...
At last he's understood..
Love makes the world go round!!!!
Thank you so much..
My friends and family..
For your love and wishes..
These are the vitamins..
Which keep me going strong!!

Struggle on and Shine

Struggle on and shine
You weren't meant to whine
Ride that slope
Don't quit
Pedal on!
You can do it!
Be strong!
Listen to God!
Discard the devil!
Enough harm you've done
To yourself!
Struggle on and shine
Make up for the time!
People have gone places
Don't stand still
Wake up! Do something!
See what you are capable of,
You've done some dastardly deeds
Stop it now!
Wake up..before it is too late
Perhaps you will not
Get another day!
Today is another beautiful day!
Be happy..feel good!
Spread the joy!
Heed the scriptures
They say it all..
This struggle between good and evil
Will go on!

Balance yourself
Like on a bike
You need to move..
Or you will fall!
Keep pedaling
Don't stall
Huff and puff
Don't give up!
You will reach your destination
Just don't give up!
Make your parents proud
Stand out in a crowd
They are not here anymore
But they would see you
From there..
When you meet them
You can tell them..
I'm sorry..I failed you
I could have done much better
I was wrong..to blame you!
Forgive me please
I wish I could have done something
That would make you proud
To be a son
Worthy of you!
Thinking of you
And all the opportunities you gave
Sadly so many
Wasted away!
I am sorry for everything
Sorry for cheating
Sorry for the lies
Sorry for the things
I did..hiding behind
Let me try and be
A worthy son

Someone you could proudly say
There...that's my son!
You both were wonderful
I think of you often
It was so sad
To see both of you suffer
I just couldn't do anything
To make you better
Thank you for everything
Everything you gave me
For all your love..
Your daily blessings
You forgave everything
Every time
I know you must have prayed
So many times
You always wished for my welfare
My well being
Some part of you both
Still shines in me
I hope I can one day
Be someone..whom you would say
That's my son!
I am proud of him!
Jagmit with tears in my eye

My Wife

She has been with me through it all
My rock..my anchor ..my support
My companion stood by me in my fall
She's the reason I still stand tall
I can make enough excuses to find fault
And perhaps some are not excuses..at all
The fact remains..on every occasion
She has stood by me..
I have many flaws and faults..
I can point them out and find them.. in all
But there is no point in that
The point is to make sure.
To be happy together..thats all!
We have everything..
We could wish for..
There is no point in squabbles..at all
So much to live for..
Let's enjoy our time together
Let's not criticize..at all
What has happened..is the past
Lets just enjoy..as long as we last
One of us will go first
It could be ..we go together..who knows
But the one that is left..
Will surely miss the other..
For we spent a lot of time..together!
We went to a lot of places
So many friends we spent time with..
Some nice memories were created..

Many photographs we took..
It is time to move forward..

With grace..
This is not a race..
But it surely is a place to cherish
Our individual space..
You do the things you enjoy
I do what I enjoy
But we make sure..
At times we enjoy together..
While we enjoy..
It is not at the cost of the other
I know you care..
And you know I care too..
There is no problem..is there?
We have a common love..
Whom we care for..
And for whom we wish
All the joy!
Here's to good health.
For you and me..
And for all those whom we love..
Let us make this place so good.
So that when we go..
We could say..
Yes..it was all good!

Happy 5th

To our sweet sweet children
And parents of Leo,
On this your special day,
Some wishes come your way!
May you both..
Be bound together..
In love..in trust..in getting to know more
About each other..
May this journey..
Be full of adventure..
May you both..
Take on all the challenges..
Together you can overcome..
Together you can enjoy..
It's much more fun..
To double the happiness..
By sharing with your..
We wish you both..
More joy..good health..happiness..
Some little troubles too..
Cause overcoming them..
Will increase the joy!
You both are our joy..
You both are the one's we love..
More than anything else..
Wish you peace of mind..
Success in all that you do..
Wish for you!

Love and respect for each other..
Some space for each other too!

Lots n lots of love..
From both of us!
5 years is a milestone..
It's just a step..to the 50th!

Staying Together

Staying together..
Has its ups and downs..
We don't think alike..
she feels..I'm not right..
An argument starts..
both try to win..
Every one loses..
The scar is born
We both stop talking..
The atmosphere gets spoilt..
Then one decides..
This can't go on..
Life is meant to be nice
Not for sulking at all!
Reason prevails
The nice things are remembered
We move on..
Knowing that we both care..
The love that stays..
Is more important..and so precious
Than a momentary phase!

Learnt from Me

You are everything I couldn't be!
You can sing and dance..
You can swim like a fish..
You are so good at your job!
Yet you say..
You have learnt from me..
I'm laid back and lazy..
Sometimes a little crazy..
But yes perhaps..
There are somethings in common
Our taste of music for one..
And the joy of simplicity..
Also we don't like boasters
We are by and large positive
And we both love playing
Scrabble..cards or table tennis
I have much to learn
First of all I must acknowledge my mistakes
Then have the strength
To overcome them
Just wanted to say..
I have the most beautiful daughter
I could ever have dreamt of
She loves me so much!!
In my own eyes I have so many flaws
She might know some
She might learn more..
But I do know..she will still love me

I just hope..
I can improve myself

Not waste so much time..
In useless pursuits..
If there was a resolution to be made
It would simply be this..
Try and not do..the things which you think
Are not good..
These are a few thoughts..
Coming as I type..
When thinking about you
And thinking about me
Lots of love..hugs n kisses
To the wonderful gift
That He has given..
A sweet and lovely Arshiya!

Leo is One

And tomorrow he's going to be one!
Though he's not a lion..
He's every bit..
As brave as one!
He's a naughty lil jolly fella..
The apple of his parent's eyes
Their life revolves around him..
The reason is clear..
He brings so much joy..
And cheer
He loves to put stuff in his mouth
That's his way..
Edible or not..
He surely doesn't care!
He knows he's handsome..
And he likes to get his way..
Loves playing a game..
Tug o war..or fetch!
He is very very fast..
And quite slippery too..
If one is not careful..
He will just..run through!
When he is unwell..
Everyone is so sad..
No one really minds though..
When his naughtiness abounds..
His likes in life..
Are very very clear..
Food comes at the top..
But very close is..
That Arshiya should be near..

So much love he gets..
And gives plenty too..
Here's wishing lil Leo
Happy happy birthday!!
And may we enjoy..
Many many more!!
We love it when he's around
Though we have to be careful
Not to leave things around!
Wishing Leo once more..
Happiness..joy..and good health..
May he love everybody..
As much as he gets!

Letter to Pitaji

I know..I made a lot of mistakes..
I'm quite ashamed of them..
I couldn't tell you about them..
But some you came to know..
However.. I'm sure you know..
I did some things right too..
I'm sure,...of those you would be proud.
I was nowhere near you...
In achievements or excellence..
I felt short..at every step.
Many times..I blamed you..
For my shortcomings..
Of course it was not right..
You knew it more than me..
I had only myself to blame..
But I was not big enough..
To admit it!
Perhaps I too..
Could have got into IIT..
Or the IAS..
But that was not to be..
I blamed you only..
For being so lenient..
And not strict!
But still..things did work out..
Eventually..
Thanks to you..
And to so many others..
I did manage..
To find a job..then got married..
And had a child.

Life moved on..
It wasn't as it should have been..
I could have done better..I know..
But I wasted away..
I was lazy..
But I will always be..
Grateful for your love and support..
Which you gave..
Unflinchingly..despite my falling short!
Now you are not there..
I Perhaps..did not..
Or was not able to convey..
My feelings..and thanks!!
For all your love..your blessings..
The pain i caused you..
How much you helped me..
Each time I fell!!

Blood Relations

Me...I am my Father's son..
Also...My mother's son..
And I have some qualities of both..
Perhaps I have some qualities..
Of my own...but not sure..
I have some..no not some..
Many bad qualities..
Which are surely my own!
I am also..my daughter's father..
And I like her qualities..
Like me..
She would have got something..
From me..and her mother..
But she's got many of her own too!
We are very proud of her..
And with good reason too!
She's caring..she's loving..
She's honest..she's nice..
She has her faults too..
But then ..who doesn't..
We are all human..aren't we..
None of us is God..
Though surely God is in us..
And we are in God too..
Cause..God..by definition...
Is everywhere..and within us all..
Without us too...
Since we are in God..
And will remain in Him..or Her..or It...
While we are alive..
And after that too..

Then Why worry!
Leave that ..we are in God's hands..
And there can be no ..
Safer place..
So..Just remember Him..
And Always..always..
Remain in Bliss!

Prodigal Son

I can identify with the prodigal son,
I've done all I shouldn't have,
But I'm coming back home again.

And like his father, my Father too,
As is His nature, forgives me,
And welcomes me back, with open arms!

It's a beautiful, joyous homecoming!
It feels good! Just hope I don't stray anymore!

Back home again,
Back home!

You and Me

I'm stuck with you,
And you are stuck with me,
Its as if we are glued!,
But its not such a bad thing,
As you care for me,
And i care for you,
Things could get better,
But it is purely upto you,
And upto me.
The years have passed by,
In a flash,
The remaining years too,
Will go by very fast,
We are here for an instant only,
Let's make our short stay,
Memorable and good,
So that we both can say,
It was a good and happy time together,
We did our bit,
To make it last!

My Name

My name is Jagmit Singh,
Of course my parents kept it,
Jag means world..
And meet means friend.
Initially it was spelt jagmeet,
Somehow I changed it,
Perhaps it was the normal spelling,
And I wanted it to be a little different,
So I made it Jagmit.
Now mit in my language,
Means to wipe or rub ..
Or to make something disappear.
Of course amongst us Sikhs,
Singh is always used as a surname.
Which means lion.
Since we do not believe in the caste system,
Our 10th Gurujee said,
All men will be called Singh,
And all women will be called Kaur.
And so my caste,
Is Sachdev,
But no one in my family uses it.
Sach means truth,
And Dev means devta,
Or a kind of God..with a small g..god.
So well,
World friend Lion.
Or World disappear lion.
Both are relevant.

The first of course is obvious.
The second is a little interesting,

It can be interpreted as ..
Though living in the world,
But not being worldly.
So not getting too influenced by material things.
And of course,
Since I am not always truthful,
And definitely not a god,
It is apt that I don't use sachdev.
A long note..on my name!
Hopefully it was interesting.

Sixty Two

Though soon I will be 62
At heart I'm just 26!
The beard is graying fast
But the hair is still black!
Till 26..I was very shy..
Now at 62..I'm getting bold
But they know..he's safe..quite old!
Life has passed by
In a flash
Who knows about the future
Enjoy each day!!

Difficult Times

When times are difficult,
Do not crib,
Count your blessings,
Which are there in plenty.
Life will always not be smooth,
There will be bumps,
Along the way,
But just as darkness doesn't remain,
There will be light,
Coming your way.
The present times,
Are difficult,
We cannot meet,
As before,
But this too shall end,
And many of those who got it,
Have got well.
This is chance for us,
To explore our inner self,
And marvel at the things,
Which we didn't notice before,
I'm reminded of my mothers words,
Whenever someone would get hurt,
She would always comment,
Shukar hai..bahut bachav ho gaya,
Meaning Thank Almighty,
It is so fortunate,
As things could have been,
Much worse.
So it is important,
To not get disheartened,

When the times are tough,
Just take heart,
From your own past,
You went through difficult times,
But they didn't last.
The difficult,
Will soon become pleasant,
And you will appreciate,
Your well-being,
All the more!

Mr Debutant

Shy I was in school..
So many pretty girls I saw..
Didn't dare to go and talk..
College may have been a little better
But still no girlfriend..to boast!
Later joined some French classes
A beautiful girl caught my fancy!
Guess I was in a euphoric state..
Said to her..I love you..at her face
Don't know what she felt..
Perhaps a shock..at the affront
Many male friends she must have had
Perhaps she felt a little twang..
At a competition in which I took part
She was a Judge..
And to my delight..
Gave me a prize..
Mr debutant..Alliance Francaise!

Son

I am my father's son
And when people say
You look like him
My heart lifts up with pride
When someone says
You look like your mother
I feel nice
As she was good and sweet
Though I am not
As good in looks
And deeds..as them
I'm really proud
Of being their son!
I could have done better
But so what
They never chided me
That's the kind they were
Never compared me to others!
They gave me love
They didn't deserve
All that pain
They got..
Just before they went
I choose to remember
The good times spent
From childhood..
To a few years ago
With them!
Their pic is by my bedside
They are my heroes alright!

I got lucky ...as hell!
That I got them..
And if ever someone says something good about me
It is all because of them!

Mama

All my life she gave me so much love,
Even now that she is not there..
Her love and memory stay..
They will not fade..
For she gave me everything..
She gave me..
My life.

She lived a good life
She was happy and spread happiness
She helped everyone
For her children..
She would do anything

She was very social, made many friends,
She was strong,
She overcame all the challenges,
Her faith was strong,
She was my mother,
All mothers are good..
But for me..
Mama was the best!

Jasleen

The eldest daughter of honorable parents
They named her Jasleen
Meaning immersed in the Lord
She made her parents proud
In every way
Music dancing and good in studies was she
In the school leaving final year exams
She came second in the entire country of Nepal
Economics honours at the best college in Delhi
Graduated with a high first division
Went on to complete MA from Delhi School of Economics
Then did her Bachelor in Education
Took up teaching..as she had tried it before and enjoyed it
Taught for more than thirty years
Principal at prestigious schools
Then quit to look after her grandkids.
Apart from an illustrious academic record
She shone on the family front
Married an Engineer from IIT
And had a lovely boy
Today she is a grandmother of two
And without being on Facebook or Instagram or the likes
Has friends all over the world
Wherever she goes,someone or the other
Comes up and meets her
All the students remember her and love her
And till now even if they are high places
Write to her and acknowledge her contribution

She's been a wonderful daughter, sister,wife,mother,grandmother,mother in law, teacher,guide to many..her sweet and friendly nature,she's got from her mother and her academic acumen from her illustrious father.
I'm writing this about her,whatever thoughts are coming to my mind,she's encouraged me for my writing and I can truly say, I'm proud and happy she's my sister.

I can trust her fully and this is my way of saying something about her.
Thank you Jasleen..for everything!

Marriage

The time to get married had come
Her parents came..
And took a look..
I saw her mother..
And presumed how she would look
They must have liked..
Something in me..
And a meeting was set up..
Consequently..
My thoughts had been..
Who would marry..a loser like me..
She was sweet..educated and intelligent..
I was eager..and liked her..
We spoke for a while
Both of us were shy..
But I guess..the time was ripe!
The marriage took place..
And we've been together
Now for decades!

Manjula

The youngest in our family
Her name is Manjula
A very very sweet baby she was
Two years younger than me
Like her sister she was good in studies
After getting a high first division in school
She too followed her sisters footsteps and joined LSR eco honours
The best college and coveted course
Secured first division in BA
Went on to do masters at Delhi school of economics
Did well there too..then took admission at Boston..
Did her masters and went on to complete her PhD
In the process marriage took a back seat
Stayed in USA for many years
Worked hard and took a job with American Express
While in the US the whole family visited her
And she was a wonderful hostess to all
Finally posted to India
She stayed with her parents
And looked after both with full dedication and love
Because of her, the rest of the siblings
Didn't have to exert at all
She quit her job when the company wanted to relocate her back to USA
And made a career switch and started
Teaching at probably the best college in the country
She's independent,dedicated and puts in her best.

Like her sister and father she's sincere.
She's helped me
in my time of need and I can trust her.
She will always come to my aid.
Some of her qualities are..she's honest to the core, she's considerate and loves her
nephew, niece and grand nephews.
This is just a small note from me..nothing that she doesn't know.Shes always
encouraged me..whatever I write resonates with her. She's been a wonderful daughter,sister and Aunt. Just wanted to express my love and thanks.

An Ordinary Man

He belonged to an ordinary middle class family
The youngest child..perhaps the brightest
A topper throughout school and college
Consistently made his parents proud
The times were tough
India was undivided and the British ruled
It was particularly tough for this family
And millions like them who were Sikhs
They were in a minority and took turns in guarding the family
India split into two..India got independent
They had to leave their home..their friends their everything
They shifted to Delhi
He got a good job
He got married
He lost his mother
He had four children
He lost his sister and his father
And he lost another sister and his brother
He rose to the top of his profession
He was one of the best in his field
One of the top Engineers of the country
He was sought after for his expertise
Even twenty years after his retirement
He was simple..he was humble
He was so so intelligent..
He was so honest..
He didn't talk ill of people
He didn't speak unnecessarily
He loved his wife and children

He invested well
He took care that many generations
After him..would live well
He was my father
He was my Hero
He was an ideal man
His father too was my hero
Was He an ordinary man?
Not in my eyes..he wasn't!!

Bauji

Such a sweet and gentle man
Full of goodness love and patience
Full of all virtues
My grandfather he was
many times told me
Akhey lagi da vey!
Meaning ..you should listen to what elders say
On some occasions he would remark
When I was being a good boy
Tu barha Biba hai!
When I grew up ..
Many times he said
Teri darhi badi sonee hai..
Your beard is very nice!
Such a caring and gentle person
No hint of ego at all
Very God fearing!
He tried to teach..all his grandchildren
Good things..Gurmukhi
And Path!
He was my grandfather!
We called him Bauji!
An epitome of simplicity and goodness
Was he!

Together

Together we became..
More than thirty years ago
Together we made a baby!
And what a sweet child was she!
Together we argued many times
Together we traveled..far and wide!
Together we looked after each other...
In sickness and in health.
Sometimes we stayed apart
But we got Together again!
Perhaps we could have done better..together
But I guess..this is how it was meant to be
We are still Together ..
After all these years
Not everyone is as lucky
We are seeing that..
Everyday!
Let's make the most of our togetherness
Lets smile and laugh and play
More often!
Let's avoid shouting and fighting..
It makes no sense..
For how long are we going to be together..
God only knows!!
Dedicated to our togetherness..
May it last long!!

Dear Father

Dear Father..
I know..I made a lot of mistakes..
I'm quite ashamed of them..
I couldn't tell you about them..
But some you came to know..
But I'm sure you know..
I did some things right too..
I'm sure..of those you would be proud.
I was nowhere near you...
In achievements or excellence..
I felt short..at every step.
Many times..I blamed you..
For my shortcomings..
Of course it was not right..
You knew it more than me..
I had only myself to blame..
But I was not big enough..
To admit it!
Perhaps I too..
Could have got into IIT..
Or the IAS..
But that was not to be..
I blamed you only..
For being so lenient..
And not strict!
But still..things did work out..
Eventually..
Thanks to you..
And to so many others..
I did manage..
To find a job..then got married..

And had a child.
Life moved on..
It wasn't as it should have been..
I could have done better..I know..
But I wasted away..
I was lazy..
But I will always be..
Grateful for your love and support..
Which you gave..
Unflinchingly..despite my falling short!
Now you are not there..
I Perhaps..did not..
Or was not able to convey..
My feelings..and thanks!!
For all your love..your blessings..
The pain i caused you..
How much you helped me..
Each time I fell!!

THANK YOU!

9 788197 770272

Printed at Repro India Ltd.